Apologies From a Repentant Christian III

EVERY STEP
WITH THE SAVIOR OF THE WORLD

Donna L. Young

WESTBOW
P R E S S®
A DIVISION OF THOMAS NELSON
& ZONDERVAN

WestBow Press books may be ordered through booksellers or by contacting:

WestBow Press
A Division of Thomas Nelson & Zondervan
1663 Liberty Drive
Bloomington, IN 47403
www.westbowpress.com
844-714-3454

All Scripture quotations were taken from the New King James Version (NKJV)® of the Holy Bible. Copyright © 1982 by Thomas Nelson. Used by permission. Hymns were taken from the "HYMNS FOR THE USE OF THE METHODIST EPISCOPAL CHURCH. REVISED EDITION." Cincinnati: POE & HITCHCOCK, 1866. Used by permission.

Cover photo was taken at the Rancho la Paloma Ministry Center in Tecate, Mexico by the author in 2019.

Interior Image Credit: Donna L. Young

Each entry embodies actual events from the author's life. Stories are shared as truthfully as memory permits.

ISBN: 978-1-6642-2220-5 (sc)
ISBN: 978-1-6642-2219-9 (e)

Print information available on the last page.

WestBow Press rev. date: 03/04/2021

Contents

~A SINNER SAVED~

~HAITI~

~THE PHILIPPINES~

~REFINEMENT~

~THE HELPER~

~INDIA~

~GERMANY & RUSSIA~

~INDIA~

~ISRAEL~

~MEXICO~

~CHINA~

~KOREA & CAMBODIA~

~RUSSIA~

~AFRICA~

Dedication

This book is dedicated to the One True Living God, Yahweh, Who alone deserves all glory.

"Father God, may You find this heart of obedience a continual, willing sacrifice and a reflection of my thankfulness, reverence, and adoration for You.

In Jesus' name, I pray. Amen."

Preface

It's been an incredible journey to walk alongside my Savior, Jesus Christ, for the past twelve years. Sometimes, the road to eternity was uncertain, rocky, and risky, while at other times, it filled my heart with wonder. With every step I took, God made sure I felt loved, protected, and wanted. I had found my sense of belonging and purpose in this life—I was made to worship the Great "I AM!"

On October 20, 2008, God saved me. For thirty-eight years, I had called myself a Christian because I wore a cross, prayed to God and attended church regularly. Yet, I lied, gossiped, and judged others without mercy. I misrepresented my God with my behavior, attitude, and words; such was my life.

In my prayers, I asked God to use my life to glorify Him but was ill-prepared for the response. I was arrested and charged with a felony! In deep and dark despair, I turned to God for help, repented of my sins, and asked Him for forgiveness. Unbelievably, Jesus Christ was right there next to me, ready to free me from the guilt of my sin. Overwhelmed with gratitude, I took my Savior's holy hand and promised never to let go.

In those first few years as a newborn believer, I blissfully and innocently sat at my Savior's feet. Back then, it was easy to enjoy the freshness and beauty of the new life Christ offered me. I had left my old sinful life behind me and felt relieved. As holiness softly crept into my heart, I felt the powerful presence of God begin to guide my every step.

And, I discovered that a new path—a path to God—will always be available to those who seek Him.

The first two years of my walk with Jesus Christ were joyous, and I wanted everyone to join me in the glorious company of my God. I couldn't wait to share my story of receiving forgiveness with the world, and so I wrote my first book, which details this miraculous testimony.

Soon after the release of the book, I was hit with a blinding revelation. Although I knew my path with God would set me apart from others, I still wasn't fully prepared for how often tears of pain would blur my vision and make it difficult to follow in my Savior's footsteps.

At times, it was perplexing to do what was right in the eyes of the LORD (Yahweh), especially when I didn't understand His plan. God didn't always provide clear signs. Sometimes, I simply had to walk in faith and trust Him to lead me. Once, I almost gave in to the temptation of returning to the familiar and sinful path of my past. Satan can be quite cunning, deceptive, and convincing! If it wasn't for God's readiness to carry me through the pain, I might have completely given up. Yet, through each affliction, God was by my side, confirming His will and blessing me for my obedience. Through His strength, I was able to persevere and continue on the path of righteousness.

During these years of occasional doubt, I kept a journal of my experiences. I wrote not only to honor and obey God but with the hope that in sharing my prayer journal, I might comfort and encourage the pilgrims who were beginning to climb mountainsides of their own. I also wanted to demonstrate how God can use our paths' steep slopes to test our faith and endurance and how, in doing so, He refines our hearts, reminding us of His sovereignty and His mighty promise to always remain with us. These journal entries then formed my second book—the last entry concluded the five-year mark of my walk with Christ.

As this fifth year ended, I was enlightened with a greater and more profound knowledge of God. I felt as though He had guided me to a glorious mountaintop. To my surprise and delight, a few broken and readied hearts were awaiting my arrival along with an encouraging message in God's Word, which said,

> How beautiful upon the mountains
> Are the feet of him who brings good news,
> Who proclaims peace,
> Who brings glad tidings of good *things*,
> Who proclaims salvation,
> Who says to Zion,
> "Your God reigns!" (Isaiah 52:7)

Gazing from atop that soul-refreshing summit, God's still, small voice inside me quietly and clearly informed me that change was ahead. No longer would I feel as though I had labored in vain. Instead, the LORD was now moving my feet firmly forward, toward those seeking sweet surrender of their own. God used me to take each person's hand, one by one, and lead them to the Holy Way. For the next seven years, God's Spirit empowered me to share the Gospel in ways far exceeding my imagination, showing me innumerable great things and unsearchable, marvelous things without number (Job 5:9).

Throughout the journey, which would eventually become this book, God created opportunities for me to share

His love. First, God let me share His redemptive message with people from all over the world while remaining in the safety of my own country. He even allowed me to proclaim the Gospel in languages I didn't speak. Later, new converts from other lands began praying for me—unbelievable!

Next, God began using me to heal shattered relationships. Incredibly, even my humble prayers appeared to bring reconciliation to a broken world. God then permitted me to "stand in the gap" (Ezekiel 22:30) for a few souls battling treacherous demons. Somehow, God's Holy Spirit, Who was living in me, had become a source of powerful protection against the enemy. Such is the thrill of faithfulness!

Privately, I still prayed that my own family members would fully surrender their hearts to my LORD. I especially prayed for my husband. Meanwhile, in another work of wonder, God enabled my husband to become our family's sole provider. For years, I had been the primary provider for my son Travis and myself. Now, God was directing LeeRoy's heart to accept my sharing of the holy gospel, a gospel my husband wasn't yet fully convinced of! Incredible!

I am aware that writing a book that honors God in the world in which we now live, may be considered countercultural. A virus is currently claiming a record number of lives, human rights protests and riots are ravaging our streets, and the pain of soaring unemployment overwhelms many. Much like in past generations, what is still needed in our upside-down world is hope and forgiveness, which can only be found in a relationship with God's only Son, Jesus Christ.

I am publishing my third journal out of obedience to God, Who recently called on me to remember His wondrous works and the abundance of His steadfast love (Psalm 106).

Donna L. Young

Not only am I writing to recall God's goodness towards me, but to ask Him to remember me for my unwavering desire to please Him and bring glory to His name (Luke 23:42).

I am also writing to encourage others to remain faithful to the works of the Holy Spirit in sharing the Gospel with this hurting world.

This book would be considerably long if I attempted to include all of the moments that God, in His incredible grace, used me to share the Gospel of Jesus Christ with another. Therefore, I've asked the Holy Spirit to guide my hand in writing stories that will bring the most glory to God.

It is my hope this book encourages you to allow God's Spirit to lead you, step by step, through even the smallest of deeds, to spread the glorious life-changing news of the Resurrection of Jesus Christ. May the seeds we plant today offer strength and hope to future generations and may our obedience to God's calling bring glory to His name as we live a supernatural life in the power of His unfathomable love.

"But you shall receive power when the Holy Spirit has come upon you; and you shall be witnesses to Me in Jerusalem, and in all Judea and Samaria, and to the end of the earth" (Acts 1:8).

Prayer

Long-awaited King and Redeemer,

I offer this book as praise and worship to You, Almighty God, Jesus Christ. Thank You, LORD, for always being a faithful guide and demonstrating that living a life filled with Your presence is the most beautiful life to live.

May every line in this book bring praise to Your holy name, and may all who read it be inspired to also,

"Declare His glory among the nations, His wonders among all peoples" (Psalms 96:3).

Through Jesus alone, I pray. Amen.

August 28, 2013

My LORD,

As I sit here today, I find myself reflecting upon the Scriptures Your Almighty Word recently opened to. For years, I have taken hold of the spine of my Bible and let the pages fall open. Recently, the pages of my Bible have, without fail, settled upon a few particular chapters that have encouraged me to write about my life-transforming journey with You.

One day, Your Spirit gently steered me to read Psalm 106. As I read, I felt You calling me to remember Your wondrous works and the abundance of Your steadfast love. A few days later, the pages of my Bible fell upon Jeremiah, chapter 17. Once again, I felt as though You had led me to the pages I was meant to read. The very first verse spoke directly to my heart. *Were You using this verse to confirm Your will for me to write with a pen of iron the stories that You had already engraved on the tablet of my heart?* I wondered. A week or two later, I read,

"Thus speaks the LORD God of Israel, saying: 'Write in a book for yourself all the words that I have spoken to you" (Jeremiah 30:2).

Out of obedience and unshakeable faith in my beloved LORD, I gathered my writing materials—my Bible, my laptop, and a stack of torn pieces of paper full of scribbled notations. Pausing for a moment, I bowed my head and began to pray.

"Father God, thank You for allowing me to walk by Your side over the past twelve years. Thank You for teaching me that the years spent committed to prayer and trusting Your will are never spent in vain. Thank You for allowing me to publish this journal as a beacon of hope for generations to come. May every person who reads this book feel a sense of renewed faith and indescribable and incomparable joy in Your comforting presence. May each reader's heart praise You as they become aware of their own miraculous story along 'The Way.' Thank You, Father, for bringing each person holding this book into my life and for guiding them to walk by my side into heavenly places.

Amen."

~AUSTRALIA~

August 31, 2013

Marvelous God,

Today, Your mercy-laden providence brought me to the side of a few distant travelers. It was time for me to make Your name known among the nations and share the great works You had done when You put me in the path of a husband and wife from Australia on vacation in Los Angeles. For some strange reason, our trailer's internet connection was taking an unusually long time to load. So, I decided to use the trailer park's shared computer situated in the park's entrance modular office.

Within a few minutes of the couple entering the temporary building where I sat, I felt the warmth of the Holy Spirit prod me to initiate a conversation. "You can use the computer if you want," I said, moving over to the couch in the lounge. The woman walked to the computer and sat down while her husband stood behind her.

Opening my Bible and settling in, I made eye contact with the woman. The frustration simmering underneath her calm exterior began to unravel. The couple wanted to visit Venice Beach, the place that Hollywood had portrayed so romantically on the "telly." Unfortunately, they couldn't find a way to get there. Sadly, they had discovered that there were no buses, cabs, or trains to the popular tourist destination.

I couldn't help myself and abruptly interrupted their conversation. "I can take you!" I offered excitedly. The woman seemed skeptical yet hopeful. Even though I tried to talk her out of visiting Venice Beach, saying, "It is full of people who are happy in their sin," the woman's mind was made up. So, I shared with my eight-year-old son, Travis, that we would be spending the day chauffeuring strangers to a famous tourist spot. We were both excited to do Your will.

In Your Son's Name, Jesus, Amen.

September 6, 2013

Good morning LORD,

Today, we all headed for the beach—Travis, our new friends from Australia, and me. The drive was smooth and easy. Along the way, we laughed over how differently we eat our hamburgers and cook on the "barbie." The husband remarked how it was odd that Americans add raw onions to their grilled burgers.

Soon, we arrived at our destination and found a "Welcome to Venice Beach" sign greeting us. We could see the excitement of our companions grow as we strolled down the world-famous boardwalk. However, a sense of uneasiness stirred within me. Vendor table after table was filled with disturbing papiermâché figurines, including many sculptures of Jesus and Mary.

As we walked along, I quietly prayed a short prayer to You with a heavy heart, "I'm sorry, God. These papiermâché idols of Jesus and Mary must hurt You very much." At one point, Travis grabbed my hand and pulled me closer. I stopped and bent down as he whispered in my ear, "Mom, I feel like turning over these tables. Now I know how Jesus must have felt seeing all the salespeople at the Temple." All I could say in response was, "I know, son. Me too!" However, I also knew that we were there for a reason. So, we continued to stroll along in peace and silence.

It didn't take long before You gently reminded me that You were by our side—as always. As we approached the next table, I noticed that a man was still setting up his display of papyrus from Egypt. I went up to the man and asked if I could hold a piece of the special paper, and he agreed. As I carefully ran my fingers down one side, I thought to myself, *Your Mighty Word was once written on this paper.* Suddenly, golden sun rays beamed through the clouds.

Smiling, we continued our walk. Before we could reach the next table, I heard the name of my Savior being sung out loud. So, I turned my head toward the music and listened carefully. A reggae artist was singing, "My Precious Jesus." I smiled and then approached the man and asked if he was a believer. He said, "Yes."

Filled with joy, I tried my best to explain the moment to our companions. They graciously remained silent. At the end of the boardwalk, Travis asked if he could dip his feet in the water, allowing me an opportunity to share a shortened version of my personal testimony with our guests. By this time, I had learned to always be ready to share my personal testimony. Now, once again, my story of forgiveness held the interest of strangers (John 4:39).

From that moment on, the mood of the walk changed to a more contemplative one. Shortly after, we returned to our car with sunburned faces and parched tongues. During the drive home, we remained silent.

Once back at the park, I dropped the couple off at their borrowed trailer. When the woman exited the car, I offered her a paperback copy of my testimony. In return, she shared her deepest longing with me: reviving a broken relationship in her life. I promised to pray to You to heal the relationship and watched her come alive as I spoke of hope, love, and life. "Jesus is waiting to take your hand," I said. Then, I prayed for the woman to believe that You are real and that You care for her.

In Jesus' name. Amen.

~NEW YORK CITY~

November 4, 2013

Father God,

One year ago, I cried out to You with a desire of reaching out to the victims of Hurricane Sandy.

Back then, I prayed that You might lead me to the East Coast of the United States to remind hurting storm victims of Your mercy and unfailing love.

Then, six months ago, I suggested to my husband that we celebrate our tenth anniversary in a unique way. *Perhaps with all the ups and downs, the two of us could take a much-needed vacation alone together. A fresh start*, I thought. But when I asked my husband what he wanted to do for our upcoming tenth anniversary, LeeRoy surprised me when he replied, "Nothing." Although I felt heartbroken at the time, I decided to trust You.

Now, I am experiencing great joy in my life. Not only will my husband and I be celebrating our wedding anniversary in a very personal way, You have also answered a prayer from over a year ago!

A few days ago, my husband phoned home from work and asked, "What do you want to do this year to celebrate our tenth anniversary?" It only took a moment for me to blurt out, "I've always wanted to see New York at Christmastime." At that moment, I had completely forgotten how I had cried out to You, approximately one year ago, on behalf of the victims of Hurricane Sandy. Back then, I prayed with all my heart, "LORD, won't You allow me to fly to New York and personally reach out to these hurting people?" Now, suddenly, New York was on the tip of my tongue once again.

My husband sighed regretfully. "How can I ever make that happen?" He said sadly.

"If it is God's will, then God will make a way," I replied. Then today, LeeRoy called home from work once more. This time, he sounded optimistic. "Sweetheart, I have to talk to you about something. My employer is sending me to Oceanside, New York."

"Wonderful!" I screamed over the phone. "Can Travis and I come along?" Dead silence. I began to smile. I knew our financial situation would not allow for two last-minute round-trip tickets to the far side of the United States. However, I also knew that with You, all things are possible!

Within the next hour, I received another call from my husband. "Our flight tickets are booked! We are all going to New York!" he said. "And, you will never believe this, but the cost of Travis' and your ticket combined was less than half of one round-trip ticket!" Apparently, LeeRoy had accumulated 50,000 points on his American Express card that the booking agent reminded him of during their call. Unbelievable!

Oh LORD, Your love is far deeper and more personal than any other love I've ever known. Thank You for days such as these that make me feel optimistic and cheerful in the assurance of Your presence.

In Jesus' name. Amen.

November 6, 2013

Beloved Messiah,

This morning, while rubbing the sleep from my eyes, my heart filled with joyful anticipation over our upcoming mission trip. Thoughts of going door to door, offering the love of the Savior, had caused an uncontrollable and childlike eagerness to flow through me.

Then during my morning devotional, You confirmed Your will. As I took hold of my Bible and allowed the pages to fall where they may, the pages remarkably landed upon a few timely verses in Isaiah, chapter 52. I began to praise You when I read verse seven:

> "How beautiful upon the mountains
> Are the feet of him who brings good news,
> Who proclaims peace,
> Who brings glad tidings of good *things*,
> Who proclaims salvation,
> Who says to Zion,
> "Your God reigns!" (Isaiah 52:7).

What an incredible privilege it is to follow at Your heels LORD, to preach the sweetness of the gospel of Christ, and to encourage lost sinners to return their hearts to You. I can't wait to do Your will.

In Jesus' name. Amen.

November 13, 2013

Sovereign God,

Thank You for how You made possible this mission trip to New York. Thank You for enabling me to reach out to others who had been cast aside, left to suffer, and forgotten. Most of all, thank You for allowing me to hold my husband's hand through it all! This past week, Your Spirit led me to humbly and gently love my husband while ministering to several broken hearts.

Just after settling into our hotel room, I felt Your Holy Spirit in my heart say, "Take your husband to downtown Manhattan to visit the 9/11 Memorial and Museum." So, I immediately approached LeeRoy and shared what I planned to do. "Since you served in the military for twenty years, I thought you might enjoy spending the day viewing a tribute, the freedom for which you fought for in a war." LeeRoy was pleasantly agreeable.

As we walked along the busy New York City streets, attempting to reach our destination—the 9/11 Memorial—LeeRoy graciously allowed me to turn my attention to those in need.

In the middle of one particular city block, several people walked by a homeless woman as though she was invisible. Seeing this caused a sharp pain in my chest. Urged by Your Spirit to respond, I approached her, placed my hands on the back of her shoulders, gently turned her around, and hugged her tight. As sweetly as possible, I whispered in her ear, "Jesus has not forgotten you... God is with you!" The woman returned my hug and wept in my arms. Afterward,

I walked back to my husband's side and took his hand again.

Not much time had passed before I felt the warmth of the Holy Spirit again. This time, He prompted me to offer encouraging words along with one of the handmade keychains that Travis and I had prepared for this trip to several NYPD officers.

Later, I met a young man who was sitting alone against a temporary construction-type barrier wall, freezing. Once again, You had coordinated a perfect opportunity for me to share Your care and concern with a hurting soul.

The young man's long hair was pulled into a ponytail, revealing the shaved sides of his head. His clothes were tattered and worn. Right away, I felt compelled to let go of my husband's hand and run to his side.

I purposely sat next to the young man. Forgoing formal introductions, I immediately asked the young man what had caused him to lead such a humble existence. Without hesitation, he began to share his heartbreaking story. "I was raised in a strict Christian home," he began. "My parents disagreed with my current lifestyle, so I had to leave. With nowhere else to go, I ended up on the streets." My heart flooded with compassion. So, I hugged the young man while tearfully responding, "Well, my Jesus has not forgotten you, and He still loves you." He instantly replied, "I know. I love Him too." His soft and sincere words overwhelmed my heart with adoration.

Afterward, I met another man who also appeared homeless. The stranger was riding on the same subway train as us. The moment we got on the train, I noticed the slumped-over gentleman. Right away, I felt Your Spirit encourage me to leave my seat and walk across the aisle to where he sat. I shared my intentions with my husband. Then, I made my way, stumbling across the fast-moving, swerving subway train.

Sitting down on the man's immediate left, I placed my arm around his shoulder and gave him a side hug. When he didn't respond to my touch, I moved my hand down his left arm and grasped his hand. I could immediately feel his icy fingertips. His gloves were ragged and torn, exposing his fingers to the cold November air.

Still, the man showed no response to my presence. So, I pressed on, "Sir, do you know what the Bible says about tired people?" I asked. Finally, a response! For a moment, the man raised his head, looking straight into my eyes; he spoke not a word. So, I continued, "Jesus says, 'Come to Me, all *you* who labor and are heavy laden, and I will give you rest'" (Matthew 11:28). The man bowed his head and slumped over even further. Therefore, I let go of his hand and slowly stood up. As I returned to my seat, I wondered if I had made a difference at all.

For the next few days, I followed Your Spirit in sharing You with those around me: a local grocery store clerk, a hardworking hotel housekeeper, and a few women we met while eating breakfast one day.

Then, today, Travis and I followed You to Staten Island, New York, to the small community hit hardest by Hurricane Sandy.

It was still dark outside when I kissed my husband goodbye. "Off to work," he said as he left our hotel room, heading for his temporary job site. Frosty air filled the space between us as I held the door ajar and waved goodbye.

After closing the door, I turned up the thermostat of our hotel room and hopped back into bed. Using a dim light, I began to spend some quiet time reading Your Word.

A few hours later, Travis opened his little eyes. Soon enough, he was full of energy and excitement, ready to devour a warm waffle breakfast. In the hotel lobby, Travis and I enjoyed a delightful, freshly cooked meal. Then, we began our drive to fulfill the primary purpose of our trip. I usually get lost driving even around familiar areas. Yet, with the help of Your Holy Spirit, not once did we lose our way in the fast-paced hustle and bustle of the state of New York.

Once on Staten Island, we stopped at the Visitors' Center to receive directions to the area hit hardest by the storm. We became instant friends with one particular employee who bundled Travis in layers of warm sweatshirts and jackets. "It's colder than you think out there with the wind-chill factor," she said, giving me a handful of jelly belly candy. Then, she told me just where to park my car and gave me a massive hug before sending us on our way.

I must say, LORD, it caught me off guard to see upturned boats still abandoned in bushes. All of the boarded-up vacant buildings caused a sharp pain in my heart. Not much progress seems to have been made this past year. *Where are these people living?* I wondered as we drove along the beachfront property. The sight reminded me of how my world turned upside down the night I was arrested and charged with a felony. Suddenly, I remembered those comforting words I heard the moment You saved me. My heart started to beat a little faster as I prepared a special message for each of the storm's victims: "Don't lose hope! God's with you."

We went from house to house, placing a keychain and candy cane against each door that remained unanswered. With the first person we met, I knew right away that You had sent us there to extend Your compassion.

He was a middle-aged man, perhaps a little older than me, who called out to Travis and me from his car. "You lost?" he asked as we began to cross the street. "No," I replied. "We're here to see you." The stranger looked at me, perplexed, as I approached his vehicle. The streets all around us were empty, giving us all the time in the world to have a heart-to-heart conversation. I cried as the man described how he had tried to outrun the deadly force of the ocean that had suddenly and dangerously filled the streets behind him. "I thought I was going to die," he said. I choked back tears and responded softly, "But you lived. God was with you then, and He is with you now. That's what we came all the way from California to tell you. You are going to get through this." Afterward, I handed the man a homemade keychain that read,

"Fear not, for I *am* with you;
Be not dismayed, for I *am* your God.
I will strengthen you,
Yes, I will help you,
I will uphold you with My
righteous right hand' " (Isaiah 41:10).

Travis gave the man a candy cane and said in his sweetest little voice, "Merry Christmas, sir!"

For the next few hours, You used my young son and me in entirely different ways. I wiped away tears with tissues and shared my testimony, while Travis, impatiently and innocently, repeated the same question. "Candy cane?" he asked, as he held out his red-gloved hand filled with dangling candy canes.

You also led us to a young Russian Catholic man with bleached blonde hair who ran a pet shop. In addition, we met a woman in her early thirties with long, curly black hair and a thick New York accent. She was overcome with amusement when we shared that we had come from California to offer her a hug for Christmas.

We also followed You to several sweet Jewish children in a Jewish daycare who looked at us with astonishment and wonder. Finally, we met a man who still lived in his crumbling home called "Stormy." I think he had turned to alcohol to numb the pain. With the smell of liquor on his breath, Stormy shared how he had remained in his top-story attic while the rising waters threatened his life and ruined his home below. My heart instantly began to ache for the elderly man. I wondered if perhaps he was grappling with more than he had described. In my mind, it was the holiday season, a time for celebration with family and friends. Yet, Stormy appeared to be utterly alone. However, through the gift of Your Holy Spirit, You used Travis and me to reassure him that he was not alone. Today, we watched as many tears of sadness were replaced with joyful smiles. What a perfect day in a not-so-perfect world!

Amen.

Psalm 93

"The LORD reigns, He is clothed with majesty;
The LORD is clothed,
He has girded Himself with strength.
Surely the world is established, so that it
cannot be moved.
Your throne *is* established from of old;
You *are* from everlasting.

The floods have lifted up, O LORD,
The floods have lifted up their voice;
The floods lift up their waves.
The LORD on high *is* mightier
Than the noise of many waters,
Than the mighty waves of the sea.

Your testimonies are very sure;
Holiness adorns Your house,
O LORD, forever."

November 15, 2013

Savior, and Friend,

Today was the last day of our New York mission trip, and it was another rewarding day, LORD, all because of You!

Just after we climbed into our rental car, I used the CD-player to play upbeat songs I had downloaded last week. While I sang along to the Christian song, tears began to flow from my eyes. From the very first word, I could see your mighty plan for the day ahead.

We drove to Breezy Point, Queens, another beach community left devastated by Hurricane Sandy. Along the way, I kept hitting the repeat button on the CD player. Soon, Travis and I were both singing the uplifting worship song at the top of our lungs.

> Wave away my yesterday
> Cause I'm leaving it behind me.
> Hello, sunshine, come what may.
> I feel something new inside me.

Even before we had arrived at our destination, an exciting hope had filled both our hearts. I hadn't called ahead to the private, gated community; therefore, I wasn't sure if we'd be allowed inside. But, again, I knew You were already there waiting for us to arrive, and I felt courageous.

After only a few minutes of waiting in the lobby area, Travis and I were invited to meet with the Principal Supervisor of the Breezy Point Cooperative. I instantly began to share my heart and testimony with the stranger. Unlike the other storm victims we had encountered, the expression on the Supervisor's face remained unchanged. He hid his feelings well behind a blank stare. "Don't cause a scene," he hesitantly said. "You can meet most of our residents in our only strip mall downstairs." Just then, the lunch siren sounded.

Within the next hour, Travis and I completely ran out of the sixty-five Christmas cards and candy canes we had brought with us. Had You orchestrated that the entire community would gather by our sides?

Even more surprising was the fact that Travis and I also left with a personalized Christmas gift. The owner of the local lumber company gave us three T-shirts to remember them by. Many people, who thought we were selling the candy canes to fund a return trip to California, offered us money. It took a while to convince the gathering crowd that we were there for them. In fact, one resident and I did cause a bit of a scene, as we both tenaciously began to bob and weave like two boxers in the middle of a ring, attempting to place a few dollars in each other's pocket. The packed crowd that encircled us, roared with laughter.

Oh LORD, every day with You is remarkable! Thank You for drawing Travis and me to this community's side. Thank You for Your generous outpouring of mercy and love.

In Jesus' name. Amen.

December 1, 2013

Mighty Protector,

It's been two weeks since we returned from our mission trip to New York City. Immediately upon our arrival, I picked up where I left off in ministering to another family here in the trailer park. At first, all was well. However, my last conversation with the husband sent chills down my spine. For the first time, I felt as though I was in the presence of a supernatural evil.

Our relationship began one day when the wife approached me here in the park. During our first conversation, she shared that her marriage of thirty years was failing. Right away, I felt Your Spirit leading me to pray with her. I offered to pray, and the woman accepted. After finishing our prayer, I returned home to our trailer and prayed again for guidance. It didn't take long before Your Spirit enabled me to recognize the practical needs of this family. Soon, I felt empowered to meet their needs.

Since the family's only vehicle was broken, I began offering the teenager rides to school in the morning. Then, when each member had started passing around the same cold, I made homemade chicken soup for the family. Almost immediately, the woman began visiting our home daily to receive additional prayer support. On a few occasions, in obedience to Your Word, I got out of bed, redressed, and stayed up late praying for her marriage (Luke 11:5-13). On one occasion, I even enlisted my husband's help, who tried his best to fix their broken vehicle. As a gift from his heart, LeeRoy offered the husband a brand-new set of tools.

After many weeks of offering love and support, one

day, recently, I felt the Holy Spirit nudge me to share my personal testimony with the husband. I watched as the man chewed on the inside of his bottom lip while I spoke. He didn't respond right away; instead, he looked off into the distance, gathering his thoughts. Then, he began sharing from his heart. Within minutes, it had become clear to me that the man was struggling with a persuasive demon that was ruling and ruining his life. "I had to kill the dog that was barking at us. My dog told me to," he said with a grim smile. Afterward, he stated that he was fine and that I should not worry about him or his family. However, it was apparent that he was not okay. Despite my confusion and turmoil at his words, every ounce of my being was telling me to allow the man to speak what was in his heart, without judging. So, I remained quiet and leaned in to hear more. When the man had finished speaking, I told him that I would be praying for him. Then, I gently suggested that he read his Bible to remind him of who he is to You and what is real. Afterward, I slowly walked away. With each step, I bowed my head a little lower and prayed.

"Father, I know that You are at work in this situation. Thank You for making known to me through their confessions how Satan is stirring up turmoil in their lives. Thank You for lending me Your eyes so that I may see Your beautiful creation in bondage and feel compassion. Thank You for allowing me to walk by their side so that they don't have to face the cunning, devilish enemy alone. Please intervene in each of their lives. Protect them from Satan's attempts to keep them in darkness and away from Your grace. And, may You, my Heavenly Father, be glorified.

In Jesus' Holy name. Amen.

~ISRAEL~

"I will bless those who bless you,
And I will curse him who curses you;
And in you all the families of the earth
shall be blessed" (Genesis 12:3).

December 4, 2013

Dear YAH,

Yesterday, I asked Travis to lead the two of us in prayer. Without hesitation, Travis grabbed my hand, bowed his head, and began to pray. "Dear Father God, I just bless You, God. You are such a good God. I just bless You. In Jesus' name. Amen."

His short, humble prayer was just long enough for me to peek at him with one eye and notice the expression on his gentle face. Travis was praying with all his heart, intending to bless the heart of the God he loved so much.

After he ended his prayer, Travis ran off to play again, leaving me to ponder the significance of those few powerful words. How could someone like me ever be able to bless the heart of such a magnificent God like You? Approximately one hour later, I found myself praying a short meaningful prayer of my own, "LORD, please send Your Spirit to guide me in seeking a special gift of worship for You, my King."

By the end of the day, I heard a whisper in my heart, "Show love and kindness to My people." I went to bed, quite curious. *How can I achieve such a request?* I wondered.

Amen.

Donna L. Young

December 16, 2013

Maker of the Heavens and Earth,

This morning, I felt a deep and tender calling by Your Holy Spirit, whispering, "Simple life. Simple life. Simple life."

Then, while His still small voice stirred my heart gently, I opened my Bible and began to read the following in the Gospel of Matthew:

"Do not lay up for yourselves treasures on earth, where moth and rust destroy and where thieves break in and steal; but lay up for yourselves treasures in heaven, where neither moth nor rust destroys and where thieves do not break in and steal. For where your treasure is, there your heart will be also" (Matthew 6:19–21).

I had just read these verses when I turned on the World News Channel. Stories about the worst snowstorm in decades to hit Israel instantly seized my heart. News anchors shared how distribution centers opened their doors to provide food, heaters, blankets, and other supplies to hundreds of elderly men and women impacted by the storm. I felt a tug on my heart. I wondered whether You were leading me in sharing Your love for this group of people near and dear to Your heart.

I opened my checkbook to examine my bank account. Once again, the balance was near zero. So, I turned to You in prayer.

"Father God, how would You like me to demonstrate

Your provision in this situation?" Soon after, I checked our mailbox. One particular letter regarding my 401K statement stood out among the rest. *I won't need this where I am going*, I thought to myself as I smiled. *Perhaps, You'll allow me to use this money to reach out to Your people in Israel with some warm blankets and heaters?* I wondered.

Then, without further thought, I immediately called my 401K plan administrator and shared my intentions. The man who took the call warned me that I'd have to pay a penalty. Perhaps by human standards, I was making a foolish decision. Yet, as a Christian, I knew that where my treasure is, there my heart will also be (Matthew 6:21). Thus, I simply responded, "There's often a cost for doing good." Next, I cashed out my plan. I immediately donated all of the money to Your chosen ones believing that it was Your desire. Within moments of writing the check, a flood of Your goodness overflowed in my heart as if to confirm that I had done Your will. So, with a grateful heart, I bowed my head and prayed,

"Father God Almighty, into Your gracious hands, I willingly place all of my resources, time, and energy. I know now that nothing upon this earth could ever offer what I have found in You. In You, I have the peace of salvation, Your Word richly dwelling in me, the strength I need to endure and do Your will, and the grace that continually draws me to Your side. Thank You, Father, for commanding me to put my faith in what I cannot see, touch, or feel. Thank You for the sweet blessing that obedience consistently brings.

In Jesus' name. Amen.

April 12, 2014

Heaven's all gracious King,

Thank You for always being accessible and for giving me the incredible privilege to approach Your throne directly.

Each time I draw near to You, You affectionately welcome me with outstretched arms. Your warmth, tenderness, and gentleness are always there to comfort me during moments of sickness, painful rejection and times when my Christian faith means facing uncertainty, pressures, and challenges. Thank You for allowing me to exchange my cares and worries for Your divine wisdom on issues that fetter my ability to trust You.

For years, I've prayed, crying out to You for divine intervention, to remove a "thorn in my side." Oh, how I wish I could remain consistent in showing others the love You have for them.

I can be even-tempered, joyous, and grateful for weeks on end, but then, without warning, I am overcome with emotional or physical pain. This pain consumes my thinking and causes a swift and sudden change in my attitude, pressuring me to speak in an unwholesome manner and give in to my emotions, mostly repressed anger.

What bothers me the most is how often the enemy uses my frailty against me, tempting me to become impatient, irritated, and self-centered. This change can even cause me to set aside the work of Your Holy Spirit at times!

Disheartened by my behavior, I seek help from Your mighty Word. I eventually recover but not before spending days on my knees in holy repentance. LORD, why must my sinful flesh continue to set itself in direct opposition to Your Holy Spirit? (Galatians 5:17).

Despite all this, I am trying to see this obstacle from Your perspective. Perhaps, You are allowing this condition to remain as a reminder of my weakness and constant dependence upon You. After all, my failures keep me humble and teach me that Your grace is always enough to lean on.

LORD, I know that I cannot escape the pain of difficult situations. Please help me to consistently rejoice in You as well as the good things You do. Help me to forgive those who persistently hold a grudge against me. Please help me to move forward with courage and victory in greater wholeness. I love You, LORD!

In Jesus' name. Amen.

June 2, 2014

Rabboni (Teacher),

Today, a peculiar thought came to mind. Seemingly, out of nowhere, I began to ponder how the women in my family once wore headscarves to church. If my memory serves me correctly, my grandmother was especially fond of a black lace floral veil. Curious, I decided to research passages from the Bible that described the significance of women wearing head coverings. I discovered that the practice of Christian head covering for "praying and prophesying" was inspired by a traditional interpretation of 1 Corinthians

11:2–6 in the New Testament. I also learned that many European countries still practice this rich cultural tradition. I immediately began to wonder if You were leading me on another adventure.

To learn more, I began watching internet videos on my computer about how to tie a headscarf. While watching one video, I suddenly remembered a beautiful red floral scarf I had owned, one I had worn much earlier, when I had worked in the corporate world. It had seemed to impress the higher-ups for some reason. I dusted the scarf and stood in front of the little vanity mirror in our trailer. Ironically, while I began putting more clothes on, Travis and the neighborhood children were dressing down. It was summertime, and we were now living in a scorching region of California during a time when wearing swimsuits and light clothing was expected. Yet, here I was, piling on more clothes. Even so, my new apparel felt natural, despite the soaring temperatures outside.

I practiced tying the scarf around my head several times. In between attempts to get the covering to remain in place, I read Your Word. I meditated upon a few of the verses in 1 Corinthians chapter eleven, which remind us that our clothes make a statement.

These days, I remain unsure of just how You might use this wardrobe change. Still, with You, I know to expect something amazing!

Amen.

June 6, 2014

Son of Man,

Today, I gained a new sister-in-Christ. For over two weeks now, I have watched as this particular woman's son played with mine in our trailer park. Even though the woman and I had said "hello" one hot day at the park's laundry facility, until today -when she came to our trailer to introduce herself and retrieve her child- we hadn't formally met.

For just under a week, I had happily added a headscarf to each daily outfit. However, for some reason unknown to me, today, I wasn't wearing the additional apparel. So, it seemed particularly odd when this stranger inquired, "Hey Donna, has God ever laid it upon your heart to wear a headscarf?" My jaw all but hit the ground! "Why yes, He has," I replied, trying hard not to imitate her southern accent. And there it was! Sweet confirmation! When I returned inside our trailer, once again, I began wrapping my head with a scarf. All the while, I thought, *Oh, how I love the way You lead me, LORD*.

Amen.

June 8, 2014

Blessed Adonai,

LeeRoy and Travis were in bed and fast asleep when I decided to watch a movie. Since our trailer's living room is also Travis' bedroom, I watched the movie on my computer with earphones. In a small little corner of the room, I cuddled up under a blanket and placed my laptop on my lap while I searched for a video. Soon, my soul was at peace in the solitude as I watched a program that had once aired on the History Channel. In the program, Holocaust survivors were sharing their personal stories of survival. I wept!

Afterward, a movie called "Anne Frank's Diary" caught my eye. More tears! When the film ended, I was still wide awake. Only now, I was eager to learn more about the stories of World War II. So, I watched another movie. Soon enough, I was hooked! I sobbed as I watched movie after movie about the Holocaust. How could I never have known about the suffering of Your chosen ones?

I must have watched four or five movies before the sun began to peek through the dark sky, by which time I felt prompted by Your Holy Spirit to search online for Holocaust survivors still alive today. *Perhaps God wants me to send a greeting card, expressing His love, to counter all the hatred Jews had once experienced*, I wondered.

With a quick Internet search, I discovered that our trailer park was only half an hour from a Holocaust Museum, where survivors regularly share their experiences. Therefore, I anxiously waited until the museum opened. Following Your lead, I called the number listed on the website. The woman who answered the phone was warm and welcoming. Thus, I shared my desire to meet one of the survivors and scheduled our first visit.

I can't wait!

Amen.

June 10, 2014

All-Sufficient Sovereign LORD,

Blessed are You, my God, my King! Thank You for another glorious day of service.

This morning, Travis and I attended our first survivors' talk at the Los Angeles Museum of the Holocaust (LAMOTH).

We arrived early and sat in the front row, just a few feet away from where the guest speaker was meant to stand. Then, we impatiently waited for the special guest to arrive. I was told that the presenter would be a woman. However, You had another plan. When the time came, a 92-year-old man, with a tattooed arm, slowly walked to the front of the dimly lit exhibit room. Right away, he began to lay out photos and documentation upon a table by his side.

Then, the older man with salt-and-pepper hair began to address the room filled with high school students. As a mother, wearing a headscarf and plain clothes, with a small child by her side, I was instantly set apart from the rest of the young adult attendees.

The man wasted no time in beginning his speech. He opened with a challenge. Perhaps he was trying to break the ice? He said, "I speak several languages fluently. Try me." One student in the crowd instantly spoke up by yelling a few words in Spanish. The guest speaker responded eloquently, and the room went silent. Then suddenly, a few words in Hebrew flew loudly from my mouth, "Baruch HaShem Adonai!" I said with great confidence. The man looked straight at me and instantly replied, "Baruch HaShem."

No one else accepted his challenge. So, after a few additional moments of silence, the elderly man began to speak about his horrific experience. He held nothing back. "I was taken to Auschwitz in my underwear. The Germans didn't allow us time to dress. Instead, they gave me a striped uniform and sent me to work in the coal mines. We tirelessly worked from sunup to sundown. If you wanted to use the bathroom, you had to obtain permission. If you didn't receive permission, you had to hold it. But the food that they gave us caused us diarrhea. Imagine having diarrhea freeze in your pants during the winter. Believe me. It was very uncomfortable. I was there only three weeks and had given up two days' rations to persuade a bunkmate to trade uniforms and jobs so that I could see my sister. She was being forced to dig into the unyielding earth. My sister was supervised by female guards with guns, whips, and German shepherds. One day, I stood by the fence and got her attention. "Do you know anything about my children?" she asked me, "My husband? Mommy and Daddy?" A female Nazi guard suddenly appeared by her side and clubbed her on the head. She fell as blood gushed. Still, the ruthless guard continued beating her.

As a young child's mother, I wanted to cover Travis's innocent ears, but how could I? What message would that convey? So, I prayed for a moment. "Please LORD, protect Travis' heart from anything that will steal his innocence."

The man continued, "I tried to rip the chain-link fence apart, yelling the only words I knew in German. Meanwhile, another Nazi guard unleashed a vicious German shepherd, commanding the dog to kill. As the dog lunged at my throat, I fought back with all my strength." Then, he paused for a moment to show the young adults in the crowd his scars. "I was mauled and left for three-quarters dead. Still, I was ordered back to work. Later, I saw two women pulling a wooden cart used to transport bodies. They picked up my sister's body and tossed it on top, like trash."

By now, I was struggling to restrain the tears, but they began to flow—a trickle at first, soon a waterfall! As the elderly man finished sharing the darkest moment of his life, I scrambled to find some Kleenex to wipe my dripping wet nose. With every word he spoke, tears of compassion continued to flow down my cheeks.

When the man had finished his entire account, many of the high-school students approached him to take a commemorative photo. Afterwards, he started to gather his photographs, memories, and World War II documentation. Finally, we were alone. I had purchased a beautiful white orchid, planted in an elegant blue pot, as a special gift for the guest speaker of the day. So, I grabbed my son's little hand and retrieved our gift from the floor. While the man placed his paperwork back into his briefcase, Travis and I approached him.

"We thought you were going to be a female speaker," I said as I handed my handpicked gift to the man. He laughed, "Nope, all man!" Then, I handed him a key chain that I had made. The key chain read, "God's with you." The elderly man looked me in the eye and asked softly, "Are you Jewish?" You should have seen the stunned look on his face when I replied, "No. I am a Christian." He admitted that he felt shocked and said that he thought I was an orthodox

Jew because I was wearing a headscarf and spoke Hebrew. "The guards considered themselves Christian too." He said. Then, an awkward pause filled the air between us. I broke the silence by sharing my testimony. Afterward, I asked, "Sir, do you believe in God?"

"No! I don't believe in anything!" He replied roughly. "My dad was a good man. How could God allow him to die the way he did… and my family?" By now, the man had become defensive and angry. However, being sensitive to the Holy Spirit, I had a strong feeling that there was more to say.

"Oh, Sir," I softly replied as I reached out and tenderly laid my hand upon his tattooed and scarred forearm. I sighed. "What if God was just showing your family mercy in preventing further torture?" He shook his head from side to side. "I don't know," he replied. Then, he mournfully hung his head. I leaned in closer and ran my fingers gently across his tattooed arm. With fresh tears in my eyes, I said, "You are God's chosen one. You are so much more than this number, the purple heart, or that police badge you hold so dear. You are the apple of God's eye." For a moment, he stopped fidgeting and made eye contact with me. At that moment, tears had filled both of our eyes. "Now, if there is anything I can do to serve you, clean your home, cook for you, anything, it would be my honor. Please do not hesitate to call me." Then, I paused for a moment to jot down my contact information.

While handing the man the torn piece of paper, I gently kissed his cheek and slowly turned to leave. For a moment, I paused and then turned back around. "By the way, what is your favorite food?" I called out. The man simply replied, "Steak. I love a big juicy steak." I smiled and turned to leave a second time.

When Travis and I returned to our car, I said a little prayer to You under my breath. "Please, LORD, comfort Your chosen one and heal his heart. Show him Your intimate love for him. Confirm that You are indeed with him. Oh, and LORD, if it would be okay, I'd like to purchase a gift card for a local steakhouse to remind him of Your deep and personal love for him."

During the drive home, I imagined the profound effect one humble gesture could have on a person's heart. At one point, my eyes welled with tears, making it difficult to see the road ahead. LORD, I love how You use me to show others Your unconditional, unwavering, and steadfast love.

Then, I said out loud, " I love You LORD!" as tears flowed freely, following the curve of my smile.

In Your Son's mighty name, Jesus, I pray. Amen.

August 3, 2014

Father God,

Recently, one day, during my quiet time with You, I realized that I was utterly exhausted, emotionally, physically, and mentally! It appears that the many years of being available at a moment's notice to share the gospel has caused me to feel quite tired. Unfortunately, I say foolish things when I'm tired!

So, I said a little prayer, "May I please take a silent retreat by Your side to rest for a while, LORD." Immediately, the phone rang.

"Hi, sweetheart," my husband sweetly said. "I am just calling home to ask if you want to take a family vacation?"

"Yes," I hollered with joy. Then, within the hour, our family had a cabin reserved in South Lake Tahoe. Thank You, LORD!

My hands couldn't have moved any faster while packing my suitcase. I packed my Bible, sunblock, my swimsuit, and a few other essentials. Soon, I was ready to go. *Straight to the cabin! No stopping to do ministry!* I promised myself.

On the way, I dwelled on how wonderful the vacation would be and how thankful I was for Your many gifts. My soul was comfortably at rest when suddenly, my husband called my attention to a growing cloud of smoke at the side of the road. Once the dust settled, we both noticed the upturned Jeep Wrangler with the driver still inside, caught in place by his seatbelt. Instinctively, my husband pulled over. I felt Your Spirit tug on my heart to assist my husband. "Stay here!" I said to Travis before LeeRoy and I ran to the site of the accident. Travis was obedient as usual and promised to pray for the man's safety.

While LeeRoy scrambled to find gauze and tape, I felt the Holy Spirit direct my feet to move toward the man still hanging upside down in his vehicle. Soon, several other highway travelers stopped to lend a hand. But when they noticed gasoline dripping near the man, they all carefully backed away. As one person called 911 for assistance, my eyes locked with the eyes of the frightened man still suspended in the jeep.

In an alarmed tone of voice, the man nervously said, "You better go too." But I knew You were with me, LORD. Therefore, I felt no fear! Instead, I grabbed the man's hand

and told him that I would not leave his side. Then, I began to pray out loud. Minutes later, the ambulance and fire truck arrived. So, I backed off and started a conversation with one of the strangers who had also stopped to help.

I said, "I am a Christian, and I believe I was placed here to pray." The stranger replied, "I am a Christian too. I will pray with you." Before I knew it, several believers gathered by our sides, grabbed our hands, and formed a large circle, begging You for help and mercy.

Afterward, LeeRoy and I returned to our truck. By then, the man had been safely removed from his vehicle. Even though the entire contents of his gasoline tank had spilled on the ground below him, the man walked away from the accident with only a minor scrape on his head! Amazing!

For the first time in years, I only shared my testimony a few times during the following few days. It was difficult to truly enjoy the time spent with my family when emergency vehicle sirens, car accidents, and police confrontations divided my attention. I had to bite my tongue in the passenger seat as my husband drove by each missed opportunity.

However, now that You have granted me a week of rest, gratitude fills my heart for a few reasons. First, I am grateful for my family and the memories You allowed us to create. Second, I am thankful for a week of rest and healing. And finally, I am grateful for Your indescribable mercies that continually move me to do Your will. Thank You, LORD, for giving my life meaning and purpose and calling me to walk by Your side.

In Jesus' name. Amen.

August 15, 2014

El Shaddai,

A horrific story is splashed across every channel of the local news and the Internet. A group of evil radicals is wiping out an ancient Christian Iraqi community. Media images show the beheading of small children in this horrific massacre.

Each day, Islamists who are driven by evil paint the letter "N" for "Nasara" or "Nazarenes" on homes in the city of Mosul. With these markings, Christians are signaled for slaughter. It is no wonder that our brethren have fled the city in masses.

As I watched the mass exodus, I couldn't help but scream out loud to You, "Abba Father." Instantly, tears began to run down my face as though I was one of the women fleeing her home with her children. Oh LORD, won't You please use me to bring hope to these hurting, displaced souls?

In Jesus' name. Amen.

September 3, 2014

Protective Father,

Recently, I learned just how You shield us.

The day had begun like any other. I had taken a short walk to the trailer park's office building to retrieve our daily mail. Right away, I noticed the handwritten, unsigned letter amidst the small stack of solicitations. Curious, I immediately opened the letter. Then, as I waved goodbye to the women in the office, I began to read. Instantly, my heart sunk deep into my chest. Someone in the trailer park had placed a hate-filled letter demanding an apology in our family's mailbox, addressed to me. Without delay, Your Holy Spirit called a name to mind, helping me to discern just who had written the letter. *How awful*, I thought, as emotional pain tempted me to wallow in self-pity.

For the next few hours, I went about my Father's business. But the ache in my chest made extending Your compassionate love with others all the more difficult.

When I finally walked through the door of our trailer, the look on my face must have caught my husband's attention. "What is going on?" he asked caringly. I didn't want to cause him unnecessary pain, so I gave him a brief account. "I have a strong feeling that the man who I recently shared my testimony with wrote this terribly hurtful letter," I said while showing my husband the envelope in my hand. A look of pure disappointment filled his eyes. "Well, I guess I'll be talking to him tomorrow!" he said. "No honey, you can't," I replied. "God's Word offers only two options in a situation like this: —forgive and pray."

A few days later, I felt Your Spirit's tug on my heart to speak with the man. So, I shared my intentions with LeeRoy. My husband quickly followed my lead and walked by my side to the man's trailer. As though nothing had happened, I greeted the man and his wife, who was standing by his side. He motioned for LeeRoy and me to have a seat at their outdoor table. There weren't enough adult-sized chairs for the four of us to sit in, so I grabbed a small child's size chair and took a lowered seat next to my husband's side. I instantly noticed the look on the man's face. A smile that he offered to my husband quickly transformed into a glare towards me.

Within minutes, their teenage son had joined us. The man spoke sharply, "My son wrote the letter." He said. Speechless, my head slumped downward. Sheer confusion! After years of serving this family, including countless hours spent praying with this young man, I was dumbfounded. I wondered, *What have I ever done to him to deserve such harsh treatment?* I was at a loss for words. The man continued. "I told my son what to write. The letter was really from me." He proudly said. At one point, I wanted to fight back by airing their family secrets. But before I could speak a word, I glanced over at my incredibly calm husband. Right away, I noticed LeeRoy shaking his head from side to side as if to say, "Don't do it." I felt like crying. Pride was telling me to defend myself, and yet, deep down, I knew what this family needed to see at that very moment was Your mercy. So, with my head held low, I endured the pain. After a few more minutes, it became clear to everyone that it was time to walk away.

When we returned home, I grabbed hold of the spine of my Bible and allowed the pages to fall open. Instantly, Your Word eased my burdened heart as You reminded me that Christ calls us to love others with a love that supersedes us, a love that is not of this world.

Thus, I closed my eyes and began to pray. "LORD, my heart hurts because of the actions of this family. Yet it is also softening because of Your great concern for me. It seems that it's possible to have your heart break and be blessed at the same time. Help me forgive them as You continually forgive me." Then, I closed my Bible and remained still.

A few days later, I decided to take our small dogs for a short walk around the trailer park. Out of respect for our neighbors, I took a different path than our usual route. Imagine my surprise when the wife approached me. She explained that something unusual had occurred shortly after our two families had met. Her seemingly healthy middle-aged husband had suddenly fallen ill and required emergency care. "Kidney stones," the woman said softly with a stricken look upon her face. My heart instantly filled with compassion for the man. "I am so sorry to hear that. I will be praying that he feels better soon," I said before slowly walking away.

Back in the trailer, I fell to my knees and cried out to You. " 'Ah, Lord God! Behold, You have made the heavens and the earth by Your great power and outstretched arm. There is nothing too hard for You" (Jeremiah 32:17). So many times, Your protection has come in the form of peace and strength in the middle of despair. But now I can see that You are also a shield that encircles me each day. Thank You, Father, that I didn't need to fight this battle. And, thank You for using this situation to demonstrate Your power, goodness, and care for me. Indeed, You are the Great I AM.

Amen."

September 22, 2014

"Lord, how they have increased who trouble me!
Many *are* they who rise up against me.
Many *are* they who say of me,
"There is no help for him in God." *Selah*

But You, O Lord, *are* a shield for me,
My glory and the One who lifts up my head.
I cried to the Lord with my voice,
And He heard me from His holy hill. *Selah"*
(Psalm 3:1-4)

Almost immediately after I accepted Your Son as my Savior, I felt the sting of rejection from others. First, I was excluded from social gatherings at work. Next, without warning, a few family members began putting distance between us. Then friends walked away. Afterward, neighbors began gossiping and acting cold towards me.

You had commissioned me to reassure others of Your mighty presence in their lives. Yet, it seems that very few were ready to receive You. Nowadays, even strangers are becoming quickly incensed with me. It's all so daily. And it hurts! *How much longer must I wait down here, LORD, before coming home to You?* I wonder.

It all began the moment I glanced out of our trailer's kitchen window and noticed an older man struggling outside in temperatures exceeding 100 degrees. Suddenly, I felt Your Spirit compel me to act quickly. At that moment, I was already ministering to several of the children who lived in campsites nearby. Although the RV park where we live has a sparkling and refreshingly clean pool, our tiny home somehow became the popular choice for any child wanting a cool break from the heat.

As seven children crammed into the space of our miniature-sized living room, I announced my departure. "Travis, I will be right back. I am just going a few feet away if you need me. Okay?" I said. Then, I prepared a cold glass of water in my favorite Coca-Cola glass for the elderly man. Afterward, I stepped out for a moment.

Guided by Your Spirit, I greeted the man with the refreshing drink in hand. Right away, the stranger thanked me. His car was stuck in the middle of the dirt road, and it would be a while before help arrived. After a few moments of exchanging pleasantries, I asked if I could bring him anything else. The man responded, "Well, I'm diabetic, and I have not yet eaten anything today." I immediately excused myself and ran back to our trailer, not only to check on the children but to prepare a homemade sandwich for the disheartened man. Within a few minutes, I delivered lunch to the man and offered to check in with him in a few days. Before I returned to our trailer again, the man graciously thanked me and commented about how he loved my vintage green Coca-Cola glass.

A few days later, I kept my word and walked over to the man's campsite. I had brought a half a dozen brand new green Coca-Cola glasses and a fresh copy of my testimony along with me. I knocked, and the man answered the door right away. After I handed him the special gift, I immediately began to share my testimony. As I spoke, I noticed a change in his disposition. By the time I had finished sharing my story, the man was on the defensive. In response, he began to speak about how he had once been part of the Franciscan Christian brotherhood. Then, he shared how he had walked away from Christianity and proudly announced how he had become a millionaire without the help of anyone else. When it was my turn to speak again, I mentioned how I had given up my weekly paycheck and began giving away all that God had provided: money, possessions, time, and energy. Afterward, the elderly man smugly began to put me down. "Well, you are stupid!" he said roughly with an air of haughtiness. "You could be a millionaire, too, if you'd stop giving all your money away." For a moment, I glanced again at the personalized gift I had just given the man. Then I hung my head low, and tearfully walked away. *LORD, through these trials, You've always been faithful. Won't You once again bring healing to my wounded soul?* I asked under my breath.

Soon after, I experienced another discouraging encounter with a stranger. One day, while playing just outside our trailer door, a man approached Travis and began to question him about why we hang a cross on our trailer. The man's forceful disposition caught my young son off-guard. Travis ran straight to my side to tell me about the stranger who had approached him.

Believing that Your Spirit had brought the man to my attention, I walked over to his trailer, parked one space away, and struck up a conversation. Within minutes, it became clear that the man who called himself a Jehovah's Witness had no intention of hearing what I believed. Instead, he merely became enraged that I didn't believe what he believed. Once again, I left a stranger's side feeling shaken and flushed with a heat rash that extended from my chest to the top of my head. Even my ears felt hot! "LORD, it's difficult to respond with grace when insults are hurled at you." I prayed.

Within the next few days, my own family members grew fuming mad at me. One day, by the power of Your Spirit, I suggested that one family member offer another grace and forgiveness. As soon as I said the word "forgiveness," years of repressed bitterness and wrath seemed to ignite again. This time, the ball of fury was hurled straight at me, not just by one person, but by several who had joined in the fight. *How could the word 'forgiveness' provoke such anger?* I wondered as tear stains marked my cheeks.

To make matters worse, and without explanation, my husband also began giving me the rejection-filled cold shoulder. At this point, I couldn't help but feel defeated. Such a vast difference from when I was in and loved by the world! All I could think to do was to bow my head and tearfully pray.

"Father God, with all my heart, I truly do believe that You have called me to be Your ambassador. Yet, each time You send me to another hardened heart, I walk away choking back tears. To add insult to injury, an onslaught of torturous thoughts seems to follow each encounter. Won't You please comfort me through Your Word?"

Then in the hopes of regaining some peace, I grabbed my Bible. I felt sure that You would raise my spirits. Perhaps You'd orchestrate that the pages would land upon a familiar, comforting verse such as Joshua 1:5-6, which says, "I will not leave you nor forsake you. Be strong and of good courage." Or maybe, the pages would fall open to Jeremiah 1:8, which says, "Do not be afraid of their faces, For I *am* with you to deliver you," says the LORD." I hoped.

But instead, the pages settled upon the enlightening words of Jeremiah, chapter 12.

> "If you have run with the footmen, and
> they have wearied you,
> Then how can you contend with horses?

And *if* in the land of peace
In which you trusted, *they wearied you,*
Then how will you do in the floodplain of
the Jordan?" (Jeremiah 12:5-6).

As I read, I felt the Holy Spirit rebuke my impatience. "These are petty troubles compared with what others suffer and what might come upon you later." He said. "Just keep a clear conscience, fear God, and be consistent in repaying good for evil. Remember that obedience flows from a heart of gratitude for the grace you have received from the Lord."

By now, I knew to be sensitive to the Holy Spirit's guidance. So, with a yielding heart, I prayed, "Heavenly Father, thank You for being my supportive, comforting, and Almighty Friend. I know that You are with me always, even in my darkest hours of hurt and sorrow. I also know that it is not Your will that even one lost soul should perish. Therefore Father, please be with each person whom You've recently led me to. Be with the elderly man who once called You "Father" but now appears to worship money instead. Be with the Jehovah's witness who does not share the same religious philosophy as me. Please be with each of my family members and neighbors who are now at odds with me. Bring Your Light to those still in darkness. Mend what is broken, heal what is sick, strengthen what is weak, and fill each heart with Your peace and love. LORD, I especially ask that You surround my husband with Your warmth and lovingkindness.

With a heart of gratitude, I thank You, LORD, for using the difficult moments of this Christian pilgrimage to prepare my heart for what lies ahead. Thank You for showing me that the darker days of my life, those filled with worry, doubt, and despair, have been permitted for Your glory. Please give me the courage to continue sharing your message of hope with this dying world. Despite future hardships or personal suffering, may each step of faith bring glory to You alone.

In Jesus' name. Amen.

METHODIST HYMNAL 1866, #519
THE IMAGE OF GOD

"FATHER of eternal grace,
Glorify thyself in me;
Sweetly beaming in my face
May the world thine image see.
Happy only in thy love,
Poor, unfriended, or unknown:
Fix my thoughts on things above;
Stay my heart on thee alone.
To thy gracious will reign'd-
All thy will by me be done;
Give me, Lord, the perfect mind
Of thy well-beloved Son.
Counting gain and glory loss, May
I tread the path he trod;
Die with Jesus on the cross,-
Rise with Him to live with God."

August 26, 2014

Son of Man,

I encountered another unusual experience today. Just after dropping Travis off at school, I noticed a man standing in front of his home, watering the bushes along the sidewalk. Right away, Your Spirit prompted me to pull up to the side of the road and strike up a conversation with the stranger, and I obeyed. Little did I know that You were leading me back to the frontlines of battle.

The man, in his thirties, was immediately kind and gracious. When he noticed that I was walking towards him, he put the hose down and turned off the water. Then, he joined me on the corner of the sidewalk. Within a few minutes, we were deep in conversation. I shared my testimony with the man. At first, he listened quietly. But then, he suddenly began to get wound up. I watched as he became jittery and began jumping up and down. Then, he started punching the air as he spoke. I didn't feel afraid, as the man didn't appear to be angry, just filled with great energy and an inappropriate way of demonstrating his excitement. "I used to be a world champion boxer!" he exclaimed loudly as he threw a right jab just inches from my face. My stomach turned into a knotted mess. I felt as though I was facing something I had never encountered before. I couldn't put my finger on it. The man appeared much like a child who had been given way too much sugar.

"*Could he be on the autism spectrum (developmentally delayed)? Was he struggling with a drug addiction? Perhaps both?*" I questioned. Then suddenly, another right hook. This time, I felt the wind whoosh across my face. *Well, if I obtain a black eye from this conversation, LORD, I am sure you will use it for my benefit somehow*, I thought to myself. As the man continued to flail his arms, my feet remained planted as though fixed in hardened cement. A strange comfort came over me. Perhaps deep down, I knew that You had led me to this man for a reason.

Then, suddenly, the man lay down upon the cement pavement. "Are you okay?" I asked. "Yes, I just need a moment," he replied. *Such a strange way to reach someone with the Gospel*, I thought as I remained by his side.

Approximately five minutes of awkward silence rolled by before I began sharing about Christ's victory over death. After I finished proclaiming the Good News, the man stood back upon his feet. By now, it was clear that he was fighting an internal battle. "I will be praying for you," I said as we made eye contact. He softly and kindly replied, "Thank you."

Upon my return to my car, I paused for a moment and said a little prayer. "LORD, I don't understand what has just occurred. Yet, I have a strong feeling that the evil one is actively involved. Please, Father, drive away any demons that may be causing or exploiting this man's struggles. Thank You for using me to stand in the gap for him today. I pray this in the name above all names, Jesus Christ.

Amen."

October 8, 2014

LORD God Almighty,

My husband returned home from work today, feeling slightly disheartened. For several years now, his employer, upon short notice, had demanded that he relocate from one jobsite to another. LeeRoy says that he has grown tired of all the shuffling around and having no place to truly call home. Even today, with his family by his side, he longs for stability.

My husband shared with me the conversation he had with his supervisor. It appeared that there would be no permanent job locations available in the foreseeable future. "I just can't keep relocating, honey," he sadly remarked. "My next assignment is in Texas. We need to be there by November 1st."

"It's going to be okay," I said, as I wiped his forehead and gave him a big hug. I could tell he was tired. My heart ached for him.

For about an hour, silence filled our trailer's cozy living room. Then, my husband broke the silence. "Honey, will you take a look at my résumé?" I was glad to support him in any way possible. So, I grabbed my laptop and began filling in the blanks. After assisting strangers day after day, it felt good to be my husband's source of help once again.

In Jesus' name. Amen.

October 26, 2014

Father God,

I've spent the past few weeks preparing for our next move. I must say that already having all that we need here with us in the trailer makes packing easier.

Today, Travis and I bade farewell to some dear Christian friends we had met in the local shopping mall two years ago.

One day, I had noticed a man seated at a table in the mall, handing out Bibles and sharing Your Word with strangers. Right away, I felt Your Spirit draw me to the table. So, I approached the man and introduced myself. As usual, I then began to share my testimony. The man introduced us to his young bride. I felt an obvious and immediate connection to the couple. Over the next couple of years, we spoke often and always greeted one another in brotherly love. Meanwhile, we prayed for each other's marriages and encouraged one another to grow closer to You.

Today, we made arrangements to meet the couple in their home for the first time. It seemed only fitting that we say goodbye in a more personal way. As we walked through their door, Travis and I were instantly welcomed by the smell of freshly baked banana bread. Then, after a few hugs and some sweet fellowship, the young woman offered to pray for Travis and me. Thus, we all grabbed hands and bowed our heads. Right away, the words of her prayer caught me off guard. She prayed, "LORD, let Donna's heart be obedient to Your call. And, if You quickly call her home to California, help her listen and return without hesitation." I remained still and did my best to absorb what was being said. In my mind, our family was permanently moving to Texas for my husband's new work assignment. I had even notified my bank, the post office, and the DMV of our address change. Therefore, I felt baffled. After her prayer ended, we hugged goodbye one last time. By the time Travis and I had returned to the trailer park, my heart had filled with bewilderment. "LORD, You are not a God of confusion. Please help me know just what to do, LORD," I prayed.

Amen.

October 31, 2014

Glorious LORD,

Today, You orchestrated an experience that brought a fresh perspective on a verse in the Gospel of Matthew which says,

"But I say to you, love your enemies, bless those who curse you, do good to those who hate you, and pray for those who spitefully use you and persecute you," (Matthew 5:44).

We had completely packed our trailer and had just finalized our last payment to the RV park when I felt Your Spirit tug on my heart to reach out one last time to the neighbor who had written the hurtful letter. Since the day I returned the man's letter to him, the man has refused to speak to me. This must have taken quite an effort, seeing that our two trailers were located only feet apart. Each day, my neighbor made it clear by his actions that his emotions were still at a boil. Remembering that I too am a sinner, I used our time apart to pray for understanding as to what the man must be going through. These prayers kept me humble and continually softened my heart towards my neighbor.

Now, Your Spirit was convicting my heart to reach out to him one last time before we moved away. So, I drove to a local art supply store and purchased a crystal glass ornament. *It is going to be Christmastime soon,* I thought. *Perhaps the man would enjoy a handmade ornament filled with a reminder of Your mercy and grace.*

Back at home, I cut out a circular piece of paper to fit

snugly inside the glass bulb. On the paper, I printed a photo that featured Travis and me with our fingers folded in the shape of a heart. Printed underneath the image were the words, "You are loved."

Afterward, I walked over to my neighbor's trailer. As I held out my hands to offer him my homemade gift, the man looked at me with surprise and wonder. His eyes welled with tears as he humbly replied, "for me?"

Oh LORD, Your promises are true! "Blessed *are* those who are persecuted for righteousness' sake, For theirs is the kingdom of heaven" (Matthew 5:10). Thank You for strengthening my resolve to continue Your work out in the world. Please help me to remember that the blessed response to hatred is always love.

In Jesus' name. Amen.

November 22, 2014

Almighty and Heavenly Father,

Thank You for Texas! I've found such immense peace here. And, thank You for the ending to my day yesterday. I stand in awe of how You used a lack of propane to lead me to a young mother living in an abandoned home with her several young children.

I was at the propane store when I heard two employees speaking about a local mother attempting to heat a roofless, abandoned home using a propane tank. She and her five children were eating out of a dumpster and living without heat or any of the essentials needed to survive.

Quietly, I prayed for the Holy Spirit to use the heartbreaking situation to bring glory to Your name. Afterward, I felt a strong desire to interrupt the two employees' mid-sentence. "Excuse me, my name is Donna, and I am a full-time missionary. I have a background in social work, and I want to help. Might you have the woman's name and telephone number? I want to give her a call."

The woman behind the counter grabbed a sticky notepad. She began to write a name and number. She said, "I am sure that the woman will not speak with you. She used to live across the street from me. That is how I know her. However, she no longer speaks to anyone, and I doubt she will respond to you either." I smiled politely and said, "It is worth a try."

When I returned to our trailer, I called the number. No answer, so I left a message. Seconds later, the phone rang. The woman and I spoke for a while before I asked if I could bring her some groceries. She agreed. Next, I called LeeRoy at work and explained the situation. For the first time in weeks, he sounded excited. "Take the $200 emergency money out of the safe and spend it on the woman and her children," he said.

I took a quick shower, gathered the money, and shared my plan with Travis. Then, Travis and I drove straight to the local Walmart. What fun we had picking out $200 of non-perishable food! When we arrived at the woman's dilapidated home, all five children ran out to greet us. While Travis and the children carried in grocery bag after bag, I shared my testimony with the woman. She began to cry and hugged me. "No one has ever done anything like this for me before," she said, trying to stop herself from showing emotion. Not knowing what was about to happen, I replied, "You haven't seen anything yet! When God breaks through the loneliness, He overwhelms you with His love!" At that exact moment, another woman pulled her truck up to the curb where we were standing. "I heard you might be able to use a few mattresses," the woman yelled, poking her head out of her driver's side window. The homeless mother broke into tears and collapsed into my arms. Her legs buckled, and I began to struggle to hold her up.

When she gained her composure, she invited Travis and me to join her inside. With no roof over the abandoned home, the inside of the house was somehow colder than the snow-covered ground outside. It was also true that they had nothing. So, I promised to bring her and her children a full turkey dinner on Thanksgiving Day. Our conversation ended with me pleading with the young mom; "Please get yourself and your children into a warm shelter. If you can't get there, we will provide transportation. And, if you can, let go of your pride for your children's sake. If someone calls you and offers to help you in the next few days, please respond favorably to their attempt." Then, I tearfully hugged the woman goodbye while Travis hugged each of the children, who were about kindergarten to high-school age. Back in our heated car, I thanked You for answering my prayer and allowing me to demonstrate the warmth of Your love for this family in need. Thank You, Father God, for such an exceptionally Spirit-filled day!

Amen.

December 3, 2014

Powerful Savior,

I received a call from LeeRoy today. While at work, he took a blood sugar test and learned that his blood sugar levels were at a dangerous stage. So, a few of his coworkers took him to the hospital. By the time Travis and I arrived, LeeRoy had already been admitted and diagnosed with type 2 diabetes. I barely had time to greet him with a kiss before the doctor returned to his room a second time. This time, she had a dietitian by her side. After providing a quick overview of a few hospital brochures, the two women left my husband's hospital room.

That's when suddenly, another visitor appeared. This time, the man was a Christian, a member of the Baptist church we had just begun to attend. I grabbed Travis's hand, and the two of us stepped out of the room to allow time for Your Spirit to speak through the man to my husband's heart.

While waiting in the hallway, I checked my husband's Facebook page. LeeRoy had already written the following message: "Well, friends and family, it has been a very rough week. I have just found out I have diabetes. This will be a new challenge in my life. The good thing is it looks like the doctors are getting it under control with the guidance of our Lord and Savior." I smiled in response while my heart filled with a renewed sense of hope.

However, within the next hour, LeeRoy privately shared his heart with me. "I want to go back to California!" he said.

Instantly, a sureness and sadness came over me. Even in the short time we had been in this state, I had grown to love Texas. Therefore, I opened my Bible in the hope of receiving some reassuring words. But, before I could read the first word, You reminded me of the prayer that was prayed over me just before leaving California. "LORD, let Donna's heart be obedient to Your call. And, if You quickly call her home to California, help her to listen and return without hesitation."

As a sweet stillness came over me, I exhaled. Soon, I was ready to follow Your lead back home to California. Thank You, LORD, for that simple prayer that revealed Your will in advance.

In Jesus' name. Amen.

January 25, 2015

Father God,

Thank You for providing for our family! Thank You for our safe return to our home state. And, thank You for LeeRoy's new job located in the Silicon Valley in Northern California. My husband is excited to no longer have to move from place to place. What's more, today LeeRoy, Travis, and I found our new rental.

For over a month now, we've been searching for a home within our budget. It seems we weren't prepared to transition from that small, underprivileged town in Texas to one of the most affluent cities in America.

Today, while exploring the local listings, a small A-framed modest three-bedroom house popped up on our computer screen.

Excited, we all hopped in the car and drove to the town where the house was located, twenty minutes to LeeRoy's work. Just as we began to peer through the windows, a neighbor from one house away approached us. "Are you guys moving in?" she asked in a cheerful voice, "You are going to love it here!"

"Well, I am not sure," I replied while clearing my throat. "We are new to the area and looking for a home near my husband's new job. Travis and I are missionaries." I was caught off guard when the woman began to encourage us even more with every word that spilled from her mouth. "Well, a super religious Christian woman lived in that home for over 60 years. She started falling, so her daughters moved her closer to them. I think you would be great neighbors. I hope you get the house," she said energetically. And with that, she returned to her home.

When the woman was out of sight, I walked up to the front door of the house. There, I noticed a door knocker affixed to the wall with the words of Joshua 24:15 written on it: "...But as for me and my house, we will serve the LORD." At that moment, I knew that we were meant to live there.

Even though today is Sunday, and most business offices are closed, we decided to submit an application. Within two hours, we received a return call. "Congratulations, you have been approved. The rental is yours. What's more, we have lowered the monthly rent by $200.00!"

"Thank You, Jesus!" I immediately said out loud.

Amen.

~ISRAEL~

January 28, 2015

Mighty One of Jacob,

When I read Scripture to my youngest son, Travis, I explain that there is a purpose behind Your Word. "Take delight in meditating on the timeless and unshakable truths of Scripture," I say.

Over the years, the two of us have experienced many enlightening moments together with You. Sometimes, You bring Your Word to life in beautiful ways that inspire wonder and deep reflection. During these moments, we praise You! Today was another one of those days.

I woke up with an urge to take Travis to a nearby tourist attraction called "The Mystery Spot." For weeks, I had been trying to teach him that Satan is well versed in trickery. Now, I wanted to show Travis just how deceptive our own eyes could be when the devil is on the prowl.

We arrived twenty minutes before the tour was scheduled to begin. We stood alongside many people at the entrance gate, waiting for their group number to be called out. Suddenly, a strange and familiar feeling overcame me as I overheard a group of young adults speaking a language that sounded like Hebrew. At one point, I was sure I heard someone say my name.

So, I peered over many heads and asked, "Excuse me, are you speaking in Hebrew? And did someone say the name, Donna?" The group of young adults, probably in their mid-twenties, quickly responded. "Yes, we are from Israel, and her name is Donna," said one group member, pointing to another. What are the odds? I said to myself. "Baruch Hashem Adonai!" I exclaimed proudly.

In the past, this phrase had always been met with a positive response. However, this time, to my surprise and embarrassment, the group remained unexpectedly silent. So, I put my head down and waited quietly for our group tour to begin.

As my son became increasingly excited, I thanked You for orchestrating the day's events. Soon, it was time for our group to witness the odd happenings at the Mystery Spot. After listening to a story about the slanted house upon the hill, we took turns exploring the inside of the sloping building. My young son innocently fell for the hoax and started to believe the silly story our group guide was narrating. At one point, I pulled him aside and said, "Things are not always what they seem, Son. Always keep your eyes upon Jesus and remember that Satan is a master at disguising things to make them look appealing." Travis simply nodded.

As we continued with the tour, I thought about how Your Word commands us to bless Your covenant Jewish people (Genesis 12:3). Then unexpectedly, I found myself standing right beside the group from Israel once again. Feeling the warmth of the Holy Spirit again, I spoke up a second time. "Do you know why God changed Abram's name to Abraham?" I asked. I had gained their attention. Each member remained silent. So, I continued on. "The "heh," that God inserted into the middle of Abram's name means grace!" All but one member of the group immediately looked down towards the ground. However, one young woman harshly responded. "No, it doesn't! It is the first letter of His name." Instantly, I felt scolded by the stranger. Yet, deep down, I knew that You were opening a door for me to speak about Your grace and mercy.

Thus, when the tour ended, with purpose in my step, I walked straight up to the group of Jewish visitors, placed my hand on the same young woman's shoulder, and asked, "May I please buy you all a souvenir to take back home with you?" The young woman looked surprised. "Why?" she asked hesitantly. "Well, you are God's chosen ones, the apple of His eye, and I am commanded by Scripture to show you love and compassion," I replied. Perhaps it was because she was recognized, accepted, and affirmed that she felt secure enough to open her heart and life's story to me.

"You mean you want to give us something just because we are Jews?" she asked. "Yes," I replied with a smile. The young woman turned her head, it appeared, to hide her tears. Once she regained her composure, she spoke about her suffering in Israel, and I listened patiently. "We are looked upon with scorn by those who are very religious. Because we are not very religious, we are seen as outsiders in our homeland," she explained sadly. At that moment, I knew that our meeting was a divine intervention.

When the woman finished speaking, I said, "God's marvelous grace is available to all who seek Him. I am going to pray for peace for you." Then, I offered her a hug. The other members of the group smiled sweetly at me. Afterward, I grabbed Travis's little hand, and we turned to walk away. Back in the car, I said a little prayer to You, "Oh LORD, You have brought Travis and me to a place called the 'Mystery Spot.' How appropriate, as Your ways, oh LORD, are such a mystery to me. Thank You for allowing me to reach out to Your covenant people today."

In the name of Yeshua. Amen.

February 23, 2015

Holy God,

Yesterday my husband commented, "It's time to stop homeschooling Travis. He needs to return to school." Out of respect for You, I quickly submitted to my husband's request and began discussing school options with Travis.

At first, I offered Travis the opportunity to attend a Christian school. "Do you want to take a break from mission work for a while and be around like-minded children?" I asked. Travis remained quiet. Therefore, I inquired further, "You will be attending chapel each morning and be around others who can encourage *you*. How does that sound?" More silence.

But, as time passed, and after praying together every morning, asking You to help us do Your will, finally, one day, Travis responded, "Mom, I want to go to public school!" Stunned, I asked, "Are you sure, son?" I couldn't tell him how concerned I was for him. However, from the brief interactions I had had with strangers around our new town, I knew that sharing the Gospel in this particular city was not going to be easy. Still, my 10-year-old son bravely and confidently replied, "If I don't share God with them, Mom, who will?" Therefore, I enrolled Travis in the nearest public school.

We both felt unstoppable as we drove toward his new school on his first day. However, we quickly learned just how far we had walked out of our comfort zone. Not even the gentlest word seemed to affect a stranger's heart. Impatience was overflowing everywhere, spurring the honking of car horns, angry tones in multiple languages, and general rudeness by both younger and older adults. How painful to go from a place like Texas, where human kindness overflows, to an area of plenty where even a smile seems to be asking for too much. Immediately, we both began to long for our Savior's warm embrace.

Amen.

~*IRAQ*~

March 27, 2015

Strong Defender,

Travis' new school seems to be weighing him down. He tells me that one particular fourth-grade classmate has been stealing from his lunch. You would think, based on Travis' description, that the other child was Goliath himself.

Every night this past week, Travis and I have prayed for You to intervene regarding this specific classmate. Still, Travis' fear persisted. So this morning, I asked my young son if he'd like me to speak to the child. Instantly, Travis seemed relieved that his mom was ready to step in and help.

We walked together down the long hallway towards his fourth-grade classroom. Then, as we drew close to where his teacher was standing, waiting to greet each child personally, I inquired, "Son, which child are you having trouble with?" Travis pointed to the child. The small child was standing among all the other children waiting to enter the classroom. I tried to hold back my smile. Of all the children in line, this particular child was half Travis' size.

Nonetheless, I approached the little boy, got down onto my knees, sat back on my heels, and looked up at him. "Hi," I said with a smile, "My name is Donna, and I am Travis's mom." The sweet petite boy with long curly eyelashes looked back at me with a look of abject terror. Even through his dark brown complexion, his cheeks turned bright red. "Travis tells me that you've taken some of his lunch lately. Does your family need food? We can give you some food if you need some." The little boy quietly replied, "No, we have food." I couldn't help but notice his accent. "You have an accent," I replied. "Where is your family from?" The boy smiled and answered back, "Iraq."

"Where in Iraq?" I asked, anticipating his response. The sweet little boy replied, "Mosul." Amazing! Covered in goosebumps, I smiled and accepted the extraordinary gift You had just given me. You had led me to a family from the exact location I had prayed for seven months ago, in the hopes of ministering to refugees.

I introduced the little boy to my son, and they shook hands, offering one another a fresh start. I asked Travis if he was going to be okay. He nodded and said, "Yes." With one more kiss and hug, I walked away with a smile on my face and a prayer in my heart. I prayed, "Father of infinite power and sovereignty over the universe, thank You for allowing me to pray to You with confidence, believing that You will hear and answer my prayers. Once again, I stand in awe of Your absolute faithfulness and infinite wisdom. Clearly, You are the ruler over all. I had asked to minister to those who were fleeing persecution in Mosul, Iraq. You answered remarkably! I didn't even have to leave the safety of my own country. Instead, You brought a hurting Iraqi family to me. Please allow me to be Your heart, hands, and feet in bringing hope and healing to this hurting family."

In Jesus' name. Amen.

April 23, 2015

King of Kings,

The past thirty days have truly been rewarding! Thank You for allowing me to share Your love and concern with this hurting refugee family from Mosul, Iraq.

Each day, this past month, the mother of three and I have met after sending off our young sons to school. Travis and I quickly learned that his fourth-grade Iraqi classmate had a little brother and a baby sister and that their family was still learning to adjust to life in the States. While his mother stayed at home with the children, his father had picked up a job as a local security guard.

For hours each day, You led me to sit alongside this

wounded, yet loving woman from Iraq. Little did I know then, just how much pain she was in.

Day after day, we sat just outside our sons' classroom on the round, hard metal lunch tables, trying our best to communicate. We struggled to understand one another. At first, the gentle-mannered woman spoke in Arabic and Farsi, while I spoke in English. Then, something extraordinary occurred. One day, we suddenly began speaking with one another in Spanish! After years as a social worker, I could hold an introductory conversation while my new friend was learning to speak Spanish from her Spanish-speaking neighbor. Unbelievable!

One memorable day after school, our family was invited for dinner to their small and modest apartment. The kindhearted woman had spent the entire day cooking in the kitchen and cleaning their cozy little home. It had been a long time since someone had served *me*. Therefore, I was eager to share a meal with them. On this occasion, LeeRoy chose not to attend. Thus, Travis and I drove straight to their home after school let out for the day. To our surprise, we were about to enjoy a Middle Eastern holiday feast!

The dining room table was decorated with a lace tablecloth and covered with delicious, homemade Iraqi food, including super crispy falafel bites, Iraqi Biryani, Bamia, Kuba, and Dolma. The bountiful aroma was intoxicating!

Sitting down at the table, I was immediately overwhelmed by the family's generosity. In the turmoil of fleeing from persecution, this small family had left everything behind, including many loved ones. Yet, even though they had very little, they were happily sharing what they had with Travis and me! Their generosity moved me to tears and surprisingly inspired me. How could I have known just how nourishing and comforting our shared meal would be? The woman's kind gesture strengthened my resolve to continue ministering to others out in the world.

A few days after our visit, I went to the local Bible store and purchased a few Bibles, Christian movies, and personalized gifts for each family member. I wasn't sure that this Muslim family would be open to Your Word. Therefore, I prayed, trusting that Your Spirit would lead my actions. Imagine my surprise when the family not only welcomed our gifts, but their faces even lit up as they held on tight to their brand-new Bibles!

"I am done with Islam!" the man said in a defeated tone, "Enough!" he added. Instantly, my heart began to ache. I knew all too well that look in his eyes. Perhaps, he also felt betrayed by the religion he had once held so dear. I moved forward and hugged the man tightly. Then I took a step backward and waited for his reply. The hurting man continued, "My religion has taken everything from me, even hope." When he finished speaking, I slid the Gospel of John DVD movie that I had brought with me across the countertop. With gratitude in his eyes, the man warmly received my gift. I tearfully smiled. "I'll be praying for you. My God loves you very much," I softly said while streams of tears began flowing down my cheeks.

Then, while Travis played with his classmate in the next room, I took a seat between the husband and wife on their apartment sized couch, just feet away from the kitchen table. "Do you understand all that has happened in Iraq?" the man questioned. "No," I innocently replied. "I am Shia, and my wife is Sunni. We had to flee Iraq for my wife's safety! They were killing all the Sunnis. My wife left her entire family behind." Tears of compassion overflowed as I glanced over at the woman. That's when my new friend smiled back at me, patiently waiting for her husband to translate into Arabic what he had just said. Soon, tears were rolling down her cheeks too. My heart couldn't contain the heaviness it was feeling, so I stretched my arms out towards the woman and embraced her. We hugged each other tightly while we cried even harder. Then, I reached into my wallet and handed her all the cash that I had. It wasn't much. Still, I thought, *Maybe she is feeling isolated and homesick. Perhaps a phone call home would assure her of her family's safety and offer some peace.* At that moment, no words were exchanged. The compassion in my eyes must have expressed what was in my heart. I placed the money in her hand while the woman sobbed.

We continued to see one another every subsequent morning. One day, I brought their family my favorite homemade dish: stuffed cabbage smothered in tomatoes and raisins. Another day, Your Spirit led me to offer gift bags filled with presents for their sweet little toddler girl. I also began to pack extra special food in Travis's lunchbox each day, hoping that he would share his lunch with his new Iraqi friend. All the while, I kept thinking about how this tragic story had turned into a beautiful reminder of Your love.

One day, just after dropping Travis off at school, I bowed my head and prayed.

"Thank You, Jesus, for making a way to reach this hurting family with the power of the Gospel. Thank You for preparing the way before me, providing the resources, and allowing me to be part of Your gracious and marvelous work.

In Jesus' name, Amen."

~CHINA~

May 5, 2015

Majestic God,

Last week, Travis began politely asking me to chaperone his fourth-grade class on a field trip to see a California Catholic Mission. For several days in a row, Travis approached me, "Please Mommy, come on our field trip with us." But I had no desire to attend. So, I simply responded, "I am sorry, son. After 23 years of working with children, I just don't think children are my calling anymore. I am so sorry. Not this time. Okay?" Travis was sad; still, he accepted my response.

Then, the day of the field trip arrived. That morning, a frazzled fourth-grade teacher approached me. "We have a chaperone stuck in traffic. He doesn't think he can make it. That means that six children will not have an adult to supervise them. Won't you please come with us? We need your help!" His kind teacher looked at me with a desperate expression on her face. Suddenly, my heart filled with mercy. "Sure, I'll help out," I replied.

Soon, we were all loaded on the long yellow school bus. Travis, his schoolmate, and I sat squished together on one of the padded rusty seats. Memories of my childhood rides to and from school, plus all those years as a summer camp counselor, flooded my mind. I was surprised when the teacher chose to sit directly behind us.

We hadn't even merged onto the freeway when I felt that all too familiar tug on my heart by Your Spirit. "Share your testimony with Travis's new fourth-grade teacher." Even though my upper lip became wet with beads of sweat and my stomach filled with butterflies, I quickly obeyed. When I finished my story, the young woman simply replied, "I was raised Catholic too. Now, I don't know. At this time, I consider myself an agnostic." I gently touched the top of her hand and smiled, hoping that the expression on my face was enough to say, "I completely understand."

Once we arrived at the mission, I was assigned my group. There I was, shepherding a small bunch of young fourth-grade boys around the exterior of a Catholic mission. I had to set aside all my feelings regarding my experience with Catholicism so that Your Spirit could work through me.

Inside the church's nave (where the congregation sits during Mass), the boys immediately scattered. Some ran up to the altar, while others headed towards the holy water fountain and began dipping their hands inside. *Time for a quick introduction to the Catholic religion*, I thought. Then, I gathered the group and explained the basics. Thankfully, my group calmed down and began to pair up, walking two by two, about the building. When one child sat in a pew and hung his head low, I approached him and sat by his side.

Suddenly, another boy in our group, who was visiting from China, came and sat down quietly on my other side. He had the most unusual, perplexed look on his face as he stared at You up on that cross. Meanwhile, the first child began to share that he regularly attended mass each Sunday at another local mission. "Do you understand what you are being taught?" I asked the young boy. The boy simply shook his head from side to side. "Don't worry. I didn't either. I am here if you need me to answer any questions for you. Okay?" The boy looked up at me with wonder in his eyes. Then, I explained how You, LORD, are most interested in a person's heart.

I was still trying to make sense of the moment when another child in our group approached the three of us and asked if we could visit other historic buildings on the grounds. He was particularly interested in seeing the jail and saloon. My giggle echoed in the hollow adobe walls of the church. "Now, tell me, what kind of missionary takes a group of children to a bar and a jail?" I said out loud. Our whole group roared with laughter.

A little while later, we did begin to stroll around the mission grounds. While we walked along, I became utterly absorbed in sharing the Gospel with each child. At one point, I became engrossed in conversation. So, when the boy from China, who was taller than me, saw a statue of You and, with great affection, yelled loudly, "Jesus Chreest! Jesus Chreest!" I nearly jumped out of my skin. Unbelievably, everyone in our group had heard the boy from China scream Your name.

Astonished, I stopped walking and began to reason with myself, "He's from China. Isn't he Buddhist?" At that moment, Travis approached me and quietly said, "Mom, we need to get the Chinese boy a Bible." Under my breath, and so that only Travis could hear, I replied, "Travis, his family is from a country that is hostile to the Gospel. I wouldn't want any harm to come to his family if they are caught with a Bible." At that moment, we both dropped the issue.

All was quiet for a few days following our field trip. No one spoke about it at school, and utter silence about the issue persisted at home as well. Then, suddenly, Travis brought the matter back to the surface. "Mom, when can we purchase a Bible for the boy from China? I think he should have one!" By now, I had to believe that Your Spirit was stirring something within Travis. So, I put aside my fears and worries and bought a Bible for the child. When the personalized Bible arrived in the mail, I tore open the box in excitement. My jaw dropped. It was the most beautiful Bible I had purchased to date! It had a soft, two-tone leather cover with the boy's name inscribed in gold lettering near the bottom right corner. Inside was Your Word, in side-by-side columns of Mandarin, his native language, and English. Now, I couldn't wait to give the precious gift to the young boy!

Before school even began today, Travis and I presented his classmate with the gift while his mother was by his side. Suddenly, the bell rang—time to enter the classroom. The boy's mother whispered something to her child in Mandarin and then took the bag with her. Without even opening the present, the boy's mother and I walked quietly, side by side, out to the school parking lot.

As we walked along, I quietly prayed, "Father God, won't You use Your Holy Spirit to enable me to speak this woman's language so that You can draw this family closer to You?"

I ask this in Jesus' name. Amen.

May 6, 2015

Savior of the World,

> "Who *is* like You, O LORD, among the gods?
> Who *is* like You, glorious in holiness, Fearful in
> praises, doing wonders?" (Exodus 15:11).

No one!

As we dropped our children off at school this morning, the Chinese boy's mother greeted me with a huge hug and tears in her eyes. At first, I didn't know what was causing her to react in such a way. But then, she asked in broken English for my email address. When I returned home and checked my email, I found a letter written through Google Translate. The boy's mother had sent me an explanation for her tears. I learned that she had accepted You into her heart just two weeks ago and that she is born again.

What's more, she had just been baptized! Such good news! I couldn't wipe my tears away fast enough.

Later, when I picked Travis up from school, several children in his fourth-grade class ran up to greet me in the hallway. "Can I have a Bible too?" they all asked, many of whom had not even been in our field trip group. Such an incredible harvest! Thank You, LORD, for allowing me to witness the divine Spirit's work in these children's hearts!

In Jesus' name. Amen.

May 14, 2015

Praiseworthy King,

Today I learned the beauty and wonder of speaking another language. Thank You, LORD, for allowing me to catch a glimpse of Your glorious splendor!

My new Chinese sister-in-Christ and I had been walking down the school hallway together in awkward silence for over a week when I decided to ask You for assistance. "LORD, please help me learn to say something, anything, in the woman's native language." At first, I wasn't sure what You wanted me to say, so I submitted the situation to You. Almost immediately afterward, I discovered a song online. Amazingly, I used to sing this particular hymn in the Catholic Church. But the version I had happened upon now was in Mandarin. Astonishing! I began to listen to the song. Unbelievably, the words were coming to me quickly, and soon I was ready to surprise my new friend.

We had only taken a few steps together this morning before I tried to speak to her. Since the words to the song were all I knew how to say in Mandarin, I spoke in English. The woman looked confused. Then, suddenly, those words in Mandarin began to flow.

> nǐ shì wǒ yī kào dì lì liáng,
> nǐ shì wǒ xún qiú dì bǎo cáng,
> nǐ shì wǒ dì yī qiē.
> nǐ hào bǐ guì zhòng dì zhū bǎo,
> wǒ zěn néng fàng qì nǐ bù yào,
> nǐ shì wǒ dì yī qiē.
>
> yē sū shén gāo yáng,
> pèi dé dà zàn měi.

As I sang, the woman gasped and sprang toward me in delight! To my ears, it was only a simple melody. Yet, the woman's surprising response caused me to wonder if perhaps Your holy accompaniment had added depth and richness to the song. I could tell that she was trying to restrain herself as she waited impatiently for me to finish singing.

Then, near the end, she wrapped her arms around me and hugged me tightly. At that moment, she couldn't explain the overwhelming effect the song had upon her heart. Your power and presence were written in her expression. "Email!" she said as we tearfully parted ways.

Curiosity immediately struck me, and I drove home a little faster than usual. While reading her translated email, once again, I was wowed! Recently, while attending a local Chinese Christian church, the woman had heard this very same song. Suddenly, I remembered that You had used this same song to capture *my* heart soon after my own surrender. Amazing!

"Oh LORD, my LORD, it's only by Your power and guidance that I can touch a heart at all. Thank You, God, for allowing me the incredible opportunity to become Your servant and child! Thank You God, for choosing me!

In Jesus' name. Amen.

~VIETNAM, MEXICO & THE PHILIPPINES~

May 22, 2015

Oh LORD, my God,

Your timing is always perfect, and Your ways far surpass all my expectations. Thank You for allowing Travis and me to witness the unfolding of Your glorious plan by returning Travis to public school.

This morning, my son and I handed out the remaining seventeen Bibles to his fourth-grade public school class. Now, his entire class, all twenty-nine children, and their teacher have a personal Bible to call their own! Some of the children have family members still in their home countries. One child is from China, another is from Vietnam, while another is from the Philippines. One child is from Iraq, while several more are from Mexico. Imagine the possibilities! The Gospel being shared all over the globe!

O LORD God, what a privilege it is to distribute Your mighty Word where it is needed most—both in the United States and around the world. Sharing this remarkable book is such a fantastic way to bear fruit and bring glory to Your name. Thank You LORD, for counting me worthy to serve You.

In Jesus' name, I offer this praise. Amen.

June 28, 2015

Perfect Restorer,

The past few weeks have been trying. It seems that the great deceiver hates a victory in Your name. Right now, he's tempting me to quit sharing the gospel. He never gives up!

Travis and I had undoubtedly reaped a harvest because, right on cue, that vengeful Satan fought back. The more I tried to remember that I was under Your divine protection, the more the tempter reminded me of how intensely and intentionally he opposes the sharing of Your Word. It's dreadful how many times he can be found throughout my story. Attacks on my finances, health, and relationships no longer surprise me, let alone how often he uses my thoughts against me!

Sadly, today, I started to believe his conniving lies. *Maybe I have failed. After all, not one person appears to have taken Your Gospel to heart. Have I done anything to impact the lives of others across the globe?* I thought as my eyes welled up with tears. Once again, the accuser was tormenting me with his fiery darts of doubt, enticing me to feel sorry for myself.

Blessed be God, You stepped in as my Savior and Friend. You helped me to recall the power of Your Word. As a result, I sprinted towards my Bible. Then before I opened Your Word, I hung my head and prayed. "Please LORD, renew my mind and calm these doubt-filled thoughts. Please help me to believe the Truth and not the tempter's lies. Guard my heart against the fear that I am failing You. I need Your help in taking another step closer to the finish line. In Jesus' name. Amen."

Instantly, a calm feeling came over me. So, I sat in my favorite chair, opened my Bible, and began to read. Through Your Word, I felt a tremendous outpouring of Your love as Your Spirit instructed me to find strength in Your constant presence. Soon, peace was restored.

Thank You, LORD, for bestowing upon me this undaunted sense of mission. Please help me always to remain committed to Your will, regardless of the repercussions.

In Jesus' name. Amen.

Postscript

After I finished writing this journal entry, I opened my Bible and allowed the pages to fall as they may. The pages landed upon Isaiah, chapter fourteen. Imagine my surprise when I read about how You will one day defeat Satan once and for all.

"Thank You, God!" I said under my breath, "for subduing Satan and for giving me rest from emotional and spiritual attacks. Rather than allowing the evil one to cause my heart to feel low today, You've allowed my heart to soar on the wings of eagles. Mighty You are, my LORD, my Rock, in Whom I trust!

In Jesus' name. Amen.

THE ADVOCATE

Charitie Lees Smith, 1863

Before the throne of God above, I
have a strong, a perfect plea;
A Great High Priest, Whose Name is Love,
Who ever lives and pleads for me.
My name is graven on His hands, my
name is written on His heart;
I know that while in heaven He stands, no
tongue can bid me thence depart.

When Satan tempts me to despair, and
tells me of the guilt within,
Upward I look, and see Him there,
Who made an end of all my sin.
Because the sinless Savior died, my
sinful soul is counted free;
For God, the Just, is satisfied to look
on Him, and pardon me.

Behold Him there – the risen Lamb! My
perfect, spotless Righteousness,
The great, unchangeable "I AM." The
King of glory and of grace!
One with Himself, I cannot die; my
soul is purchased by His blood;
My life is hid with Christ on high, with
Christ, my Savior and my God.

~ITALY &
THE PHILIPPINES~

July 18, 2015

Father God,

Over the past few months, I have endeavored to model my faith in You upon children. Today, I find myself praying for stillness, asking You to help my heart to remain at peace in believing that I have obeyed Your will.

One morning, I received an unexpected call from a sweet ten-year-old girl. We first met this adorable child from the Philippines sometime during the year before when the little girl and Travis had been in the same fourth-grade class together. "Can Travis play today?" the child innocently asked. "Yes, of course," I replied. Soon, the little girl with shiny, long black hair was on her way to our home.

The petite child and her mother were still new to the USA. Each time I heard their wonderful accent, I felt as though I was transported to the Philippines-joy overflowed from my heart.

After she arrived at our home, another child who lived down the street from our new rental knocked upon our door. The young boy and his family had recently moved to the States from Italy. Seeing that his parents and I both came from traditional European Catholic backgrounds, it didn't take long before we established a comfortable friendship. Also, there were very few other boys to play with around our new neighborhood. So, Travis and this Italian child were an obvious match as buddies. He was ready to join in the fun for the day.

As we were experiencing blistering summer weather, the three children quickly came up with a plan. "We want to build a lemonade stand," they said. As a result, I scrambled to gather and lay out glue, boxes, markers, and a poster board for them to create their masterpiece. Meanwhile, I busied myself in the kitchen, juicing tons of lemons and inventing a refreshing drink for thirsty pedestrians.

Since we currently live on a bustling street, and the house directly across from us is under construction, I had no doubt that the three children would have a busy day. And indeed, the lemonade stand was a hit! In my heart, I thanked You as I watched the three young children from entirely different cultures, ethnicities, and parts of the world play together in joy and love.

After that, the two young children visited frequently, finding peace and joy in our home. One day, I felt Your Spirit softly nudge my heart and remind me that You bring others to our side to learn about You. I knew to obey the Holy Spirit's prompting. So, during the next play date, I shared my testimony with the little boy's parents. Afterward, I shared the same forgiveness story with the little girl's mother. Over the following weeks, I watched my son play alone. All calls regarding playdates had ceased. Perhaps it was the sorrow on my sweet son's little face that caused my mother's heart to shatter. Thus, I made sure to allow plenty of time for those one-on-one moments with Travis to alleviate the bitter sting of rejection. Meanwhile, I trusted that You were at work in the hearts of these two families.

Oh LORD, each time that feelings of isolation cloud our path, You are quick to remind us that You are always with us, even in our hurt and sorrow. Today, we will hold close to Your promise to heal our hearts and offer us the strength we need to continue to reach out to others.

In Jesus' name. Amen.

July 27, 2015

My LORD, my God,

Today, as I sit with Your Word resting upon my lap, I find myself reflecting once again on Your sovereign hand that led to my marriage to LeeRoy. *Where would my marriage be today without You?* I wonder.

At times, it was hard to follow Your instructions on the best way to respond to my husband. With strangers, You had led me to share my personal testimony and the glory of the Gospel. However, at home, I was to win my unbelieving husband through a consistently gentle and quiet spirit (1 Peter 3:1-4). In my heart, I still dreamt about the joy my husband's final and complete surrender to Your Son, Jesus Christ, would one day bring.

Today, I experienced a very precious moment when You allowed a rush of glorious memories to flood my mind, reminding me of the many times that You had sent other Christians to assist me in reaching LeeRoy's heart.

One day, my husband went golfing. His regular golf buddies were busy, so he thought he might golf alone. But, that day, You sent another golfer to walk by his side for the entire eighteen holes. When LeeRoy returned home from his round that day, he couldn't wait to announce that the other player was a Pastor from a local church. In a way that I could never have, the Pastor had shared his love for You with my husband.

On another occasion, while tensions at my husband's job were rising, You sent a Christian coworker to my husband's side. My husband and the Christian man shared a small office space. One day, my husband watched his Christian coworker read Your Word during lunchtime. Unbelievably, LeeRoy returned home excited about how he had begun to read the Bible at work.

And today, I learned that some of my husband's internet acquaintances are sharing the Gospel with him. Through each spiritual story, my husband is being reminded of Your incredible forgiveness and mercy.

Dear LORD, my heart is overcome with gratitude. Thank You for Your amazing, wondrous ways! Thank You for continually working hard behind the scenes, for showering my husband with Your sweet grace, and continuously sending other believers to my husband's side in an attempt to turn his heart toward You. May the seeds that each believer has sown inspire faith in my husband so that Your will may be done here on earth as it is in heaven.

In Jesus' mighty name. Amen.

August 04, 2015

Glorious Creator,

Righteous are You, LORD, for You have allowed me to confide in You regarding the burdens of my heart. Today, my heart fills with utter sadness. Therefore, I've found a quiet resting place to sit beside You now.

This past week, two of the people I had been praying for passed away. I felt certain You'd answer my prayers for a full recovery for my friend's adult daughter. And, I felt sure that You'd also spare the life of the little eight-year-old girl who had gone missing. For weeks, I poured my heart into each prayer, while strong feelings of comfort assured me that You would respond in a positive and uplifting way. I was at peace, and without hesitation, I submitted my prayers to You.

First, I prayed for my friend's daughter to be healed of her brain tumor. Then, I prayed for the missing little girl to be returned safely to her family. With immense sorrow, this past week, I learned that my friend's daughter had passed away. Not possible!

Then on the very same day, police found the body of the little missing eight-year-old girl! Why LORD? Why? The horribly sad news caused me to feel helpless and powerless. Thus, I ran to Your side.

"All-powerful God, I am wondering why a community is left to mourn the little girl's brutal murder? And, why is my faithful friend's heart shattered at the loss of her daughter?" You said,

"And whatever things you ask in prayer, believing, you will receive" (Matthew 21:22).

I prayed, believing! Yet, the woman and the young girl still passed away. Oh, Father and mighty Savior, I know that Your ways are higher than my ways. Please help me to trust Your plan when my prayers do not line up with Your will. Thank You for allowing me to withdraw to a quiet place to find repose in You. As I lean into You now, I feel Your consoling touch wiping away my tears.

LORD, if it is Your will, use me as a source of ease and encouragement for these two mothers who have suddenly and unexpectedly lost their daughters. I ask this in Jesus' name.

Amen.

~A SINNER SAVED~

August 22, 2015

"I say to you that likewise there will be more joy in heaven over one sinner who repents than over ninety-nine just persons who need no repentance." (Luke 15:7)

Savior and Friend,

For the first time today, Your Holy Spirit led me to someone who was seeking sweet surrender of their own. Miraculous!

It was late this evening when my computer made a noise. LeeRoy and Travis were already fast asleep. So, in the peaceful quiet, I decided to write to You in my online journal. That's when an old childhood friend sent me a greeting over the Internet. Ding! I nearly jumped out of my seat. Sometimes, even a faint sound can startle me while deep in thought.

At first, we chitchatted for a few minutes; a sentence here, a sentence there. Then, my childhood friend made it clear that she was in desperate need of hope. Initially, I tried to listen and be a good friend. But then, I wanted to offer her the hope that I had found in You. Amazingly, I felt bold and brave. Therefore, I courageously typed, "...have you asked Jesus to come into your heart? Do you want to pray with me right now?" To my shock and amazement, my childhood friend immediately replied, "Sure."

Thus, I began to type the following: "Okay, pray this prayer with me. Dear LORD Jesus, I am in great need of peace. The peace I hope to find in You. I know I am a sinner, and I ask for Your forgiveness. I believe You died for my sins and rose from the dead. Jesus, please help me to know You, trust You, and follow You as my LORD and Savior. Guide my life, Jesus, and help me to do Your will. I place my heart into Your hands. In Your Holy Name, Amen." Next, I hit the send button and waited a few moments through the silence for her reply.

A few minutes later, ding! "Amen. Thank you, Donna. No one has taken the time to help me," she responded. "Oh, sweetheart, I am always a phone call away," I wrote in reply. "I have lost myself," she answered back. "Actually," I wrote, "If you prayed that prayer, according to God's Word, You have just been found!" Then, I offered to send her a personalized Bible chosen especially for her. She graciously and sincerely thanked me before she ended our conversation. In my mind, I pictured my childhood friend walking away with a freshly cleansed heart and a new life in Christ.

Oh LORD, moments like this keep the flame of hope in my heart alive and make me anticipate what tomorrow might bring. Thank You for allowing me to witness the radical transformative miracle of Your love on a sinner's heart. Most of all, thank You for being the One who never leaves a soul behind. I love You, LORD!

Amen.

~HAITI~

September 21, 2015

Holy Father,

Thank You for this morning. A funny thing happened just after I placed my Bible aside-I felt my heart fill with Your awe-inspiring joyfulness. So, I looked to You for my next task. "What can I do to worship You today, LORD?" I asked.

Without hesitation, a thought came to mind causing me to remember the week You saved me.

One night, back in 2008, I found myself captivated by a television special about the country of Haiti. That night, I prayed, "Please God, use my life to bring others to You." Since I had participated in mission trips before, I really felt that You might send me on another short-term mission, perhaps this time to Haiti. However, a few days after praying that heartfelt prayer, I was arrested and charged with a felony. In a jail holding cell, I surrendered my heart to You.

Now I smile as I notice the Haitian-born mailman, who had recently been assigned to our street for delivery, suddenly approach our street. As he parks his work vehicle in front of our neighbor's home, I instantly feel a strong urge to reach out to the man. Not knowing what to say, I would rely on the Holy Spirit's help to guide my words.

From our living room window, I could see that the man was struggling to sort the jam-packed containers of mail in the back of his mail truck. Because of the sweat on his brow and the weary look on his face, I could tell he had been laboring for quite awhile. *Perhaps he'd appreciate a cold drink of water*, I thought to myself.

Then, just as I heard him roll up the noisy aluminum back door to his mail truck, I quickly ran to the refrigerator, grabbed a cold bottle of water, slammed the front door of our home behind me, and walked over to the man. "Haiti, I am praying for you," I said, holding out the bottle of water in front of me. Since his first arrival, I had addressed this particular mailman as haa-EE-ti (Haiti) because that was where he was from.

On the first day we met, we made a quick connection. Just as I had done so many times before, I shared my testimony with the stranger. But unlike many times in the past, I felt even more excited to share my story with this particular man. Perhaps this was because I had been watching that special on Haiti the day I had prayed for You to use my life for Your glory. Now, after all these years, You had brought Haiti right to my door step.

During that first meeting, the kind, tall, and married man shared his story too. "Haiti is very different from the USA," he said. Then, he spoke about his disappointment in his current position as a United States mail carrier. "I have a Master's degree. I can't believe I am *just a mailman*. All my life, I've waited for, dreamt of, something more. Now, I am living my American dream, and still, I feel empty," he stated in a defeated tone. "You are not alone. I felt the same way the night I prayed for God to send me to Haiti," I replied as I handed him a copy of my book. We unexpectedly became friends that day.

On days when the temperature outside was hotter than usual, Haiti would use the garden hose in our front yard to wet his head and cool off. Meanwhile, I'd share Your love for him by always having a cold bottle of water waiting for his arrival. Each time my new friend inquired about You, my eyes welled with tears, and gratitude filled my heart.

Thank You, God, for using me during these precious moments to nurture this loving Haitian man's faith. The gift of Your grace humbles me! Although I was a colossal sinner, a liar, gossip, and judged others without mercy, still, You forgave me. Somehow, You now count me worthy to serve You. Therefore to You, my King eternal, immortal and invisible, Who alone is wise, be all the honor and glory forever and ever. (1 Timothy 1:12-17).

Amen.

December 19, 2015

Trustworthy Guide,

Today, I took hold of my Bible's spine as usual and allowed the pages to fall open as they may. The now thin, worn pages settled upon the sixth chapter of Jeremiah. Right away, the tenth verse caught my eye.

> "To whom shall I speak and give warning,
> That they may hear?
> Indeed their ear *is* uncircumcised,
> And they cannot give heed.
> Behold, the word of the LORD is a reproach
> to them;
> They have no delight in it."

Instantly, I began to wonder how You might incorporate this verse into my day.

It has been almost one year since our family moved to the Silicon Valley in California. I know it sounds strange, seeing that I was raised in California, but this area of the state seems so different from what I am used to. I suppose each part of the world has its challenges. Still, living here feels as though *I'm* the outsider. Sorrowfully, those living here seem to have no use for the power of Your name, except to use it in an argument.

In our new city, even the smallest transgression is cause for insult and belittlement. For instance, the other day, while driving my car across town, I was stopped by a bicyclist. Surprisingly, a complete stranger had ridden his bicycle up to my car's side and yelled, "Pull over." Thinking that the man might need help, I immediately pulled to the side of the road. Imagine my surprise when the man then parked his bicycle alongside my car, then leaned in closer towards me, and said, "Jesus would have signaled!" Instantly, I was taken aback. I thought I must have heard him wrong. Out of disbelief, I said, "I'm sorry?" The bicyclist smugly repeated, "Jesus would have signaled." The man then proceeded to belittle me about my driving skills.

At that moment, I felt sure that the cyclist only sought an argument for argument's sake. Rather than quarrel, I remained calm and simply replied, "I'll try to use my indicator more in the future." My response must have surprised the man. Because afterward, he quickly peddled away.

Unfortunately, hostility and anger seem to be common emotions here. In fact, this past year has been incredibly challenging for Travis as a few of the boys at his new middle school have made him the target of bullying. Both of us have often gone to bed feeling discouraged.

One day, feeling especially weary, I reached out to my Pastor's wife for prayer support. Wouldn't you know it, immediately after she prayed, Travis, my faithful sidekick, appeared by my side. His presence was just what I needed to encourage me to press on in ministry. Within the next few hours, Travis and I had assembled over forty "Bible goodie bags" in an attempt to reach out to the lost children of his new middle school—just in time for Christmas Day!

Afterward, I met with Travis's new principal and requested that we be allowed to distribute our gift bags. She shared with me that she feared retribution if she allowed Travis and me to hand out Bibles on campus. Instead, she suggested that Travis and I stand on the adjacent street corner. Therefore, just before school let out for the day, Travis and I took our place on the closest street curb and awaited the final school bell.

Unbelievably, after only about ten minutes, Travis and I had distributed every last Bible! We also handed out over forty Christmas cards. Children were still asking for Bibles when the last goodie bag had been handed out. My heart warmed when one particular child, who had seen what we were offering, timidly asked, "Can I please have a Bible too?" I frantically searched my car for a bible track, a torn piece of paper with a scripture, anything I could find in the cracks and crevasses. All along, I prayed, "Please LORD, I need one more Bible." Remarkably, I found another Bible in the back of the trunk of my car. As quickly as I could, I attached a candy cane to the top. The boy's smile said it all!

Later, when Travis and I returned to our car, I paused for a moment before opening the driver's side door. An inexpressible and glorious joy filled my heart while warm tears dropped one by one onto my feet below. I thanked You for a fantastic ten minutes of my journey with You.

Then, before bedtime, I walked out to my car to double-check that the windows were rolled up. Rain had been forecasted. While walking back to our doorstep, my eyes caught a lit sign affixed to our town's tallest skyscraper. "Peace on Earth," the sign read.

"Oh LORD, even in a world filled with darkness, the brightness of Your perfect glory still shines!

Thank You LORD, for restoring peace to my heart and for reminding me that Your peace which surpasses all understanding, guards my heart and mind through Christ Jesus (Philippians 4:7). I am so grateful for You!

In Christ Jesus, Amen."

January 11, 2016

Holy God,

Along this journey, You have introduced me to many people suffering from the afflictions of horrific circumstances, broken relationships, physical sickness, and addiction. Every time I trusted You and obeyed Your Spirit's promptings, small miracles occurred. Recently, I have been sensing that You are calling me to others who are being tormented in a very different way. Today was one of those days.

I was only one block away from reaching my destination,

the grocery store, when I noticed a woman slumped over on the cement curb. The woman was wearing worn, tattered, and dirty clothing. So, I immediately thought, *Perhaps she is homeless.*

Then, as I went about my regular weekly shopping, prompted by the Holy Spirit, I added a few extra items to my grocery list to offer to her. Soon, it was time to leave. I prayed that she would still be sitting across the street when I exited the grocery store. Happily, she was. So, I parked my car in the adjacent church parking lot and approached the sleeping woman.

At first, I received a friendly response. But when I offered the woman a large bottle of filtered water, she looked at me with disappointment. She said she couldn't drink the water because it was probably contaminated. So, I offered her the other grocery items that I had hand-picked, especially for her. The stranger reached out her hand and reluctantly accepted the rest of my gifts.

For a moment or two, we made light conversation. I shared my testimony with her, and as most people do, she listened politely. She then began to share a Scripture with me. For a split second, I was convinced that she was a Christian too. Then, unexpectedly, the look in the woman's eyes turned sinister. "Let me tell you about God," she said, as she sprang up and threw her hands in the air. In an instant, the peaceful moment between us had utterly changed. "I believe in God," she added, now screaming for everyone to hear. Then, she began to quote even more Scripture; only this time, she was twisting Your Word. What's more, she was adding a few curse words for emphasis. I tried to quiet the woman down by sweetly and peacefully quoting the Scriptures correctly. But this only made her shout louder still. "What was happening?" I questioned. For a moment, I felt as though I was battling the devil himself.

I was caught off guard, yet, by this point, I was aware of some of Satan's tactics. So, I wasn't at all worried. I also knew that the Holy Spirit would offer me the gift of discernment to recognize and distinguish whether demonic forces were coming for me. At that moment, I stayed and allowed the woman to continue raging.

Just as he had done on many occasions before, the evil one made every effort to scare me. Even so, I felt as though the power of the Highest God was protecting me. So, with the assistance and guidance of the Holy Spirit, I remained strong enough to withstand her curse-filled rant. My heart ached for her when she said, "There I was, in jail, no one to care for me. I cried out to Satan and said, 'if you take away this pain, you can have my soul.'" Before she could finish speaking, tears began to stream from my eyes. Just then, I had a feeling that I shouldn't engage in a prolonged conversation. So, in response, I said, "God's with you, and I will be praying for you." Then, I slowly walked away, questioning if I had done enough to demonstrate the depth of Your love, mercy, and forgiveness.

Later on, as I reflected on the day, I sat silently in Your presence. I had to fight against the anxiety I felt each time I pondered how to demonstrate lovingkindness to someone battling mental illnesses or gripped by sin and controlled by Satan.

Through You, I had learned how to overcome evil in my own life. Now, I needed even more courage to shine Your image in the minds of those battling the invisible war raging around them.

Please, LORD, help me know just what to say and do in these uncertain and unfamiliar circumstances. As I share in the pain and suffering of those whose demons have chased them to the streets, please shine Your brilliant radiance through me and help instill hope in each person again. Thank You for using me as Your light to defeat the darkness of this world.

In Jesus' name. Amen.

March 7, 2016

Abba Father,

Thank You for always remaining by my side and for encouraging me at precisely the right moment.

Recently, I began to identify with the prophet Isaiah when he said,

> "Then I said, 'I have labored in vain, I have
> spent my strength for nothing and in vain;
> Yet surely my just reward *is* with the LORD,
> And my work with my God'"(Isaiah 49:4).

I had somehow begun to focus on how I could not shy away from the difficult relationships surrounding me. *Was I making a difference at all?* I wondered as doubt and gloom began to overwhelm me. Today, I received a message over the computer that inspired me to press on in sharing the Gospel with this hurting world.

The message was from a young woman whom I had met

over four years ago. I had all but completely forgotten how Your Spirit had led me to reach out to her.

One day, while ordering a breakfast treat for Travis and me, I heard Your Spirit whisper, "Reach out to the pregnant teenager who is working the drive-thru shift." It was an extraordinarily frigid and frosty morning when I stretched out my hand to offer her my bank card. Her hands were all but frozen. "Can I buy you a warm cup of coffee to wrap your hands around?" I asked, "Or I can go buy you some cozy gloves?" The young woman politely refused. Just then, Your Spirit led me to share my testimony with her as she rang up my order. A few days later, I ran into the same young woman and shared with her that I had been praying for her. This time, we made a connection.

A few weeks later, the same young woman moved into the apartment next door to where Travis and I lived. As soon as I found out that she had moved in, I walked up the stairs to her apartment. I left my home phone number on a slip of paper at her doorstep. "Call me if you ever need anything," the note said.

Right away, the young lady called, and we spoke for quite a while that day. During our conversation, I shared that Travis and I would be moving soon. Right then and there, I felt Your Spirit move my heart to offer her my apartment-sized refrigerator. When I shared my intentions to provide her with the used refrigerator, she began to cry. Then, she said, "We need that so much right now!" I began to tear up too. "Just remember that God is with you and always will be!" I said in reply.

Fast forward to today. Discouraged and feeling as though I was not making much of a difference for Your Kingdom, I opened my inbox and began to read my messages. Imagine my surprise when I read the following.

"Hi Donna, I'm not sure if you remember me. I met you at my job. I was about four months pregnant, and you had pulled up and seen that I was distressed, so you prayed for me. Every time I saw you, you were always so nice to me. And then, when I was about eight months pregnant, me and my daughter's dad moved into an apartment next to yours. You gave us your fridge, and you also gave me a copy of your book. I just want you to know that I still think about you and your kindness and how you would tell me everything will be alright… My daughter and I are doing great, and I'm living a better life because I found God."

After reading her sweet message, I sat in my kitchen chair for a while, thinking about her kind words. Streams of tears rolled down both cheeks. The story she told exceeded my hopefulness without fail! I looked up to the heavens and immediately thanked You.

Deep down, I knew that I didn't deserve credit for her words of gratitude. All I had done was learned to listen to Your Spirit and follow His prompting. When He compelled me to act, I simply obeyed without questioning Him. You alone deserve all the glory.

Oh LORD, You have taught me to be anxious for nothing, but in everything by prayer and supplication, to come to You with a thankful heart (Philippians 4:6). Thank You for allowing me to bring my doubts and insecurities to You. I suppose what I needed was a reminder that the same gracious God Who forgives sin, mends broken hearts, redeems lives, and bestows mercy has somehow deemed *me* worthy to serve Him. Perhaps I may never know the effect a kind deed has had on another person's heart. Yet, You know. And, that is all that matters after all.

Amen!

"The Spirit of the Lord GOD *is* upon Me,
Because the LORD has anointed Me
To preach good tidings to the poor;
He has sent Me to heal the brokenhearted,
To proclaim liberty to the captives,
And the opening of the prison to *those who are* bound;
To proclaim the acceptable year of the LORD,
And the day of vengeance of our God;
To comfort all who mourn,
To console those who mourn in Zion,
To give them beauty for ashes,
The oil of joy for mourning,
The garment of praise for the spirit of heaviness;
That they may be called trees of righteousness,
The planting of the LORD, that He may
be glorified."(Isaiah 61:1–3).

~THE PHILIPPINES~

March 26, 2016

Almighty God,

The narrow trail that I am on has recently become crowded by hundreds of people from the Philippines. *How many will remain after they hear the Truth?* I wonder.

I had spent the past forty days preparing for the hope-filled day of Resurrection Sunday by prayerfully submitting my heart to You. As a result, Your Spirit's still small voice inside began making it clear that I was meant to joyfully share the Gospel of Jesus Christ through my computer.

Since one of the ways I can best reach others overseas is through Facebook, I decided to place an ad on my page, welcoming everyone to hear my testimony. Today, I took a deep breath and curiously opened my Facebook Author page. *Perhaps someone has seen my ad*, I thought. Imagine my shock when I noticed that over 1,000 people from the Philippines had seen and responded to my Facebook page. The sheer number of people who had personally reached out increased so rapidly that I felt ill-prepared to respond.

At first, it was challenging to keep up with the increasing number of Catholics rushing to my side to learn more about Your Son and His marvelous ways. Yet, my foundation of trusting in You was firm. Therefore, I felt sure that You would use my words to respond to each person personally. Perhaps, You might use my Catholic background to reach a wounded heart.

Before I could even write the first reply, Your Spirit led me to remember a man I met back in 2012. One day, a stranger from a call center in the Philippines reached out to me regarding my book's possible publication. During that first conversation, in my usual manner, I had shared my testimony with the man. Then, I explained that my book had already been published. Strangely enough, the man continued to call. It was during these subsequent calls that we became friends.

Therefore, when he asked for a copy of my book to share with others, I quickly responded. I mailed several copies to him without hesitation. One day, my friend sent his reaction to the words you had used my hand to write. In a Facebook message, he said, "Hello Donna. After I read the book, it touched me. And I can't wait to distribute it to people who badly need to read the book. I myself didn't expect to feel the way I felt after reading it. Honestly, I cried coz I can relate and felt so sorry for what I thought was right before. Especially the letter from Dad. Indeed, I was so blinded before." Wow, thank You, God!

My friend continued to live in the Philippines, and as such, provided the perfect avenue for conversations with others. Through overseas phone calls and in divine appointments here in the States, I often commented in discussions after hearing that wonderful accent by asking, "Are you from the Philippines? I have a friend who lives in Cebu City."

"Ah!" the person would excitedly reply. Then, our dialogue would instantly become very friendly and agreeable. Afterward, the rest of the conversation became another opportunity for me to testify to Your goodness and mercy.

Today, I find myself enjoying the warm feeling of contentment that has spilled into my heart. Over the years, I have experienced both the highs and lows of Christian ministry. It is true that a life lived following You can be challenging at times. Yet, when we submit our lives to the works You have uniquely called us to, joy can always be found.

In Jesus' name. Amen.

~REFINEMENT~

May 3, 2016

Way Maker,

A few days ago, I watched an inspirational movie called "Little Boy." By the time the film ended, I was in tears. Through this touching movie, Your Spirit had convinced my heart that my prayer life needed Your rejuvenating power.

In this inspirational movie, a little boy is teased incessantly by his peers for his small size. One day, he attends Catholic mass with his mother. During the mass, a priest says,

"So Jesus said to them, "Because of your unbelief; for assuredly, I say to you, if you have faith as a mustard seed, you will say to this mountain, 'Move from here to there,' and it will move; and nothing will be impossible for you." (Matthew 17:20).

Instantly, the little boy is swept up by the idea that if he has enough faith, his best buddy, his dad, will return home from the war and repair his shattered heart. And so, he prays with all his heart. As I watched this, I could feel the little boy's hopefulness fill my heart too.

Suddenly, I felt an urge to revisit my prayer board. As I gazed upon the shiny white plastic wipe board, I thought about the many names I had once erased. Out of impatience and a fading belief that You'd reply, I substituted a few names for others. Now, seeing those wipe marks disquieted me.

So, without reservation, I removed that little wipe board from our bedroom wall. *Perhaps a sincere prayer life, though faded, isn't lost forever*, I thought, as I grabbed a dry erase marker and wrote those names a second time. "LORD, please return my prayer life to its once lively state," I prayed. Amazingly with each name I rewrote, I felt a spark of hope warm my heart again.

Amen.

May 8, 2016

Heavenly Father,

This past week, I fervently prayed that You'd sway the hearts of each name that I had rewritten upon my prayer board. I prayed, "Please Jesus, help them seek Your presence." Today, You reminded me that You still hear my prayers and are willing to respond!

Travis and I had just pulled up to our home's curb and parked my car when my husband drove his truck into our driveway. By his side sat our loved one. In Your perfect timing and plan, and after many years of a strained relationship between her and me, now, as an adult, she was suddenly returning for a visit.

She walked straight over to greet me. It had been a terribly long and painful absence; now, it was as though none of that mattered and all had been forgiven. Without hesitation, she reached out to me and wrapped her arms around my shoulders. A sincere hug! Then, we all walked inside the house together. While putting my purse away in my bedroom, thoughts raced through my mind. Rather than give in to doubt and fear, I bowed my head and began to pray, "Please LORD, help me to be warm and affectionate towards this family member. I trust Your Word that says, with even a mustard seed of faith, I can say to this mountain, 'Move from here to there,' and it will move (Matthew 17:20). Our loved one seems to need Your loving touch now. Please remove the mountain between us so that I may graciously lead her to Your side.

I humbly ask this in Jesus' name. Amen."

May 9, 2016

Loving LORD and loyal friend,

I must say, after so many years of prayer and uncertainty, and even with the tension surrounding hurting hearts, it's nice to have another female in our home. With so much distance between us, I had all but forgotten just how kind, funny, and thoughtful this young woman could be.

My husband has now gone off to work and left the two of us to find our way together-she in one room and me in the other. Insecurity and hesitation from years of rejection have come over me. So, I've decided to step back and focus my attention on ministering to others instead. Please help me, LORD, to navigate this reunion. I don't want to disappoint You. But, I am afraid.

In Jesus' name. Amen.

May 12, 2016

Glorious God,

First, let me apologize for allowing fear to direct my steps during my loved one's current visit. I realize now that You wouldn't have brought her to our home without wanting me to attend to her hurting soul. Today, I read Your Word, which says, Your righteousness goes before me. Your glory is my rear guard and that I am not to fear (Isaiah 58:8). Therefore, I've decided to take her out to lunch. She says she likes Vietnamese food, so I've decided to surprise her and take her to a restaurant in a unique town nearby called "Little Saigon." Please, LORD, be with both of us during this uncomfortable time. Help me do what is right in Your eyes. Allow Your Holy Spirit to guide the words between us so that together, we might bring glory to Your name.

Through Jesus, I pray. Amen.

June 24, 2016

Sovereign Savior,

It feels as though years have passed since the last time I wrote to You. So much has happened since then that I've hardly had time to digest it all.

First, our female guest returned home after her two-week visit with us. We had the most delightful time together! Thank You for the grace that flowed in every conversation since that first lunch get-together. Thank You for healing our relationship; indeed, truth was spoken in love.

Immediately following her stay, we heard another miraculous knock at the door. A second answered prayer from my revitalized prayer board! A different loved one asked if he could stay with us for a few days. Another pleasant visit! When he left, more loved ones suddenly appeared. With so many unexpected visitors whose names were written on my prayer board, my head was spinning. Many years of distancing and rejection were coming to an abrupt end as several people who had once refused to be around me suddenly drew near. With tears streaming down my face, I whispered, "Thank You, God.

Amen."

June 25, 2016

Everlasting Father,

I was eager to read Your Word this warm, sun-drenched morning. As I reached for my Bible, I noticed the delightful sound of the chirping birds outside. My heart was chockfull of satisfaction from how I handled recent visits from others. Without a doubt, I believed that You were waiting to offer me immediate positive and uplifting feedback.

I took hold of the spine of my Bible and opened Your Word. Suddenly, the pages flipped like an old movie projector before landing upon Ezekiel chapter thirteen. Clean white sheets with unfamiliar verses stared back at me. I began to read. However, I couldn't fathom that the pain of consequence was headed towards me, ready to overwhelm.

Very quickly, a shockwave of conviction ran through me, causing me to sit motionlessly. I began wracking my brain. I contemplated every recent conversation and interaction I'd had. What could I have done to displease You? I couldn't see it! Sinking deeper in my chair, I bowed my head and tearfully repented.

When the tears stopped rolling down my cheeks, I decided to turn on my computer. Perhaps Your saving grace would enable me to walk through the painful moment. I allowed the Christian music station to choose the song. Suddenly, a particular worship song began to play. A waterfall of tears resumed its course when I heard myself singing along with the words. "I see the things You do through me as great things I have done." You were convicting me of hidden sin. Still, I remained blind, so I prayed, "Oh, Father, I am not sure how I have stepped out of Your will, but my sin appears to be hurting You. Please take away my pride. Help me see my secret faults. Humble me gently, LORD.

Amen."

June 26, 2016

Good morning Father God,

Today, I awoke to an incredible sense of peace. So, I joyfully grabbed a cup of coffee and reached for my Bible. Then, just before allowing the pages to fall open, I optimistically ran my fingers over the cover. *It's going to be a good day*, I thought. After all, I had repented.

Then, I opened my Bible. The pages settled quickly upon Daniel, chapter four, an all too familiar story! *Oh, no! A story about how pride comes before the fall*, I instantly thought. Then, before reading Your Word, I began reading my personal notations written in the margins.

I tried to force myself to stay calm, but my head was now shaking involuntarily from side to side. "Another day filled with bewilderment and sadness," I said to myself as I slumped over in my seat. "I am sorry, God! I am sorry! Amen." I repeated out loud.

When I had finished praying, I noticed the time. Sunday morning church service would be starting soon. Surprisingly, my husband, who typically plays golf on Sundays, decided to attend church with our 11-year-old and me. It had been some time since LeeRoy had accompanied us to a church service. However, in my sorrowful state, I had a difficult time fully grasping the moment.

Even so, I wanted LeeRoy to know how much I appreciated his company, so I shared my heart's concern out loud. "God is correcting me," I told my husband, "and my heart is hurting." My eyes welled with tears. "But I am so glad that you decided to come with us today," I said. My husband smiled and grabbed my hand. It felt good to have him by my side as we walked along toward the main church building.

Once inside the sanctuary, I tried to put on a happy smile. But it didn't take long before the tears began to flow again. "Let's turn in our Bibles to the book of Revelation," the Pastor suggested. Then, he began reading chapter two. I followed along with my finger, brushing the pages. Suddenly, an old sense of doubt and fear began to grip me again. *My sin is too great! And my walk with You is too crooked, LORD*, I thought. My heart began to ache as I wiped the flow of tears upon the sleeves of my sweater.

After the service had ended, I walked hand in hand with my husband out to our car. My head hung low. In my heart, I prayed, "Holy and righteous Father, please help me understand exactly how I have displeased You so that I may repent and turn from my sin. Cleanse me from my hidden faults.

Amen."

June 27, 2016

Almighty God,

This morning, I found myself quickly running to Your side. Like a child seeking her Father's approval, I opened Your Word praying, begging, that You would reveal Your heart to me and restore my relationship with You. "Please, Father, tell me what I have done. Amen," I prayed.

Then, I nervously opened my Bible. The pages landed upon Psalm four. One verse leaped off the page. "How long, O you sons of men, Will you turn my glory to shame?" (Psalm 4: 2). Once again, I burst into an awful fit of tears. Just as suddenly, I bowed down and placed my forehead upon the floor. For quite some time, I allowed the tears to pool below.

When I finally found the strength to rise from the floor,

I decided to reach out to a mature sister in Christ. I shared my burden with her. "God is mad at me," I said, "and I don't know what I have done to upset Him. Perhaps, I'd be better off just getting an ordinary job. I seem to be failing at being an Evangelist."

"God is not mad at you, Donna," my loving friend replied. Then, she prayed that You'd console my doubt-filled heart.

Afterward, I went about my day. I fought every minute against the desire to go back to bed and hideaway. It was a long, painful, and weepy day.

Amen.

June 28, 2016

God Almighty,

Before opening my Bible today, once again, I poured out my heart to You through prayer. I prayed, "Father, I know that You love me enough to bring my sin to the surface and that You are always quick to forgive. Won't You please open my eyes and reveal those thoughts, behaviors, and words that are sinful in Your sight? Help me to turn from these ways. This I pray, through Your only Son, Jesus. Amen."

Next, I opened my Bible. Amazingly, You had orchestrated for the pages to land upon Isaiah, chapter forty-eight. With a humbled heart and fervor to hear Your response, I began to read. My eyes immediately came to a screeching halt upon reading a few verses.

"For My name's sake I will defer My anger,
And *for* My praise I will restrain it from you,
So that I do not cut you off.
Behold, I have refined you, but not as silver;
I have tested you in the furnace of affliction.
For My own sake, for My own sake, I will
do *it*;
For how should *My name* be profaned?
And I will not give My glory to another"
(Isaiah 48:9–11).

In an instant, You had opened the eyes of my heart. Suddenly I could see my prideful response to those recent visits from others. At that very moment, I realized that I had allowed self-confidence to fuel my foolish pride. I completely missed how You had offered miraculous breakthroughs for each person's name written on my rejuvenated prayer board. Not only that, but in my heart, I had also taken credit for the things You were doing through me. I was stealing Your glory! Now, I felt sick to my stomach.

With my head bowed low, I said another heartfelt prayer: "Almighty God, please forgive my propensity towards pride. It seems that I've had to confess this ugly sin to You far too many times. Yet, each time that I submit my heart to Your grace, asking forgiveness, You allow me to walk away feeling restored yet again. LORD, if I have learned one spiritual truth since the beginning of this journey with You, it is that my flesh will betray me and that in Your goodness, You are always willing to forgive! Thank You, LORD, for Your righteous judgments!

Also, thank You for reminding me of Your role in my

life and for allowing me to remain by Your side as Your humble servant. Once again today, my heart is only about You, and all I want to do is reflect Your goodness.

In Jesus' name. Amen.

ISAIAH 12

"And in that day you will say:

"O Lord, I will praise You;
Though You were angry with me,
Your anger is turned away, and You comfort me.
Behold, God *is* my salvation,
I will trust and not be afraid;
'For Yah, the Lord, *is* my strength and song;
He also has become my salvation.'"
Therefore with joy you will draw water
From the wells of salvation.

And in that day you will say:

"Praise the Lord, call upon His name;
Declare His deeds among the peoples,
Make mention that His name is exalted.
Sing to the Lord,
For He has done excellent things;
This *is* known in all the earth.
Cry out and shout, O inhabitant of Zion,
For great *is* the Holy One of Israel in your midst!"

June 29, 2016

El Shaddai,

This morning, I woke up feeling grateful. You had used failure to do some spiritual housecleaning, and through it all, You remained strong and sure by my side. After many days of tearful repentance, I was hoping to receive Your comforting Word.

I took a deep breath, closed my eyes, and opened my Bible. Then, I peeked open one eye and glanced down at the pages. The bold heading immediately caught my attention, and soon I was smiling again! The pages had landed upon 1 Samuel, chapter nine. Sheer relief! You were greeting me with a story about the humble start of Saul's ministry. With a smile beaming upon my face, I began to pray the following:

"Heavenly Father, thank You for looking into my heart and showing me that which was displeasing You. Thank You for loving me enough to discipline me. Thank You for using Your refiner's fire to purify my heart. LORD, thank You for never rejecting me, even when I cause You pain. And, thank You for using Your Word to comfort me today. Once again, I passionately place my heart back into Your hands. Please, LORD, help me always remember that the work You have called me to do is not about me. I know now, 'living a life that brings YOU glory is the most glorious life to live' (Anonymous)." In Your mighty name, Yahweh, I pray.

Amen.

~THE HELPER~

September 5, 2016

Father God,

This morning has been wonderfully quiet and still. Left alone to my thoughts, I've begun pondering the magnificent work of Your Holy Spirit.

In October 2008, I surrendered my life to You, and just as Your Word promised, that day, Your Spirit took up residence within me. Through repentance, I have begun a sweet fellowship with Him. His work in me has made living worthwhile!

During those initial steps, following the lead of Your Spirit simply meant that I was saying "yes" to those promptings and warm goosebumps that, to me, indicated I was supposed to act upon goodwill towards others. Most times, others responded positively, as though You had prepared each response ahead of time. Inevitably, I'd walk away, my face beaming from having felt Your divine Spirit working through me.

Further down the road, however, a sweeping and robust change occurred. Nowadays, a call to action triggers an unsettling physical response, fear. Instead of that warm, comforting, and exciting sensation, these days, Your Spirit's promptings consist of a nauseating feeling accompanied by a racing heart and moist hands that set my feet in motion.

At first, the intense and stressful, gut-wrenching feeling troubled me. But now, I embrace those moments when my palms become sweaty, and my stomach fills with butterflies, not knowing the cost. After all, I've learned that when I obey Your Spirit's prodding, there's no limitation to what Your love can do!

Today, I would like to thank You for allowing Your love to conquer the impossible. I would also like to thank You for the gift of Your gentle, sensitive Holy Spirit, Who continually equips me in serving You and leads me in bringing glory to Your name.

Amen.

~INDIA~

November 3, 2016

Father God,

For the past few weeks, I have felt a strong desire to return to a part-time paid position. Many years of frustration arising from hearing that same question, "So are you working?" has caught up to me.

I must admit that my emotions were running high at the thought of returning to a traditional job. Once again, my role as a missionary had been challenged. This time, in haste, my husband had hurled an accusation my way. "You don't get paid to pray," he said, while pointing his finger at me. After years of hearing the allegation that what I did didn't matter, I decided to quiet those opposing voices once and for all from friends, family, and even acquaintances. Thus, I hastily sat at my computer and searched for a job. Oh, my distrustful heart!

It didn't take long before I found a position that worked around Travis' school schedule. Not to mention, the job sounded almost too good to be true! In an introductory email, the woman looking to hire additional help wrote, "The man we take care of is a monk who never accepted money for anything. When his writings started being published, he wanted all the proceeds to be given to India's orphaned children. He has since established a home for seventy children who would surely have perished otherwise." Wow!

The elderly man's assistant explained that the aging man had recently experienced a massive stroke and required personalized care. "You would be a 'backup' caregiver in the case of an emergency," she explained. I was looking forward to meeting with her.

On the night of my interview, I drove deep into the mountains to meet the man in need of care. I was quickly greeted at the door by the woman who had sent the email. The woman and I sat at the dining room table for almost thirty minutes, sharing our stories. As usual, I shared my testimony with her. Then, she shared a bit of her life history with me. She spoke about the emotional pain she was currently experiencing. Just as I was ready to shake her hand and accept the position, the woman said, "Well, I'd like you to come meet the client. Will you please follow me?" Instantly, we left the dining room area and walked into the front bedroom where the man was laid upon an electronic hospital bed.

The elderly man was in the middle of a garment change. At first, I turned my head to the side to offer him some privacy. Then, after he was covered and dressed, I looked towards the man once again. I will never forget the look on his face: sheer terror! From the very second our eyes locked, a dreadful and nervous look filled his eyes. I couldn't help but wonder what had caused his reaction. What had this particular man seen in me? Could it have been Your resurrected power? No one else seemed to notice his wide-eyed panicky glare. Neither one of us said a word.

Thankfully, the woman who was conducting the interview broke the silence and proceeded to share with me the truth about the situation. She revealed the real parameters of my role as his caregiver. My part would be very different than what I had been promised earlier. As a result, I politely declined the position.

Before I left that night, I shared the Gospel with this hurting woman. I then prayed that she would be brave enough to say "Yes" to Your invitation of forgiveness and love. Afterward, I prayed that she'd be obedient in sharing the gift of eternal life with this helpless, dying man. Before my long drive home, I called my husband and shared all that had just occurred.

Then just before bedtime, I said another prayer. I prayed, "Oh LORD, I need discernment and Your reassurance. In the light of all that has happened tonight, I am left wondering if the enemy is taking great care in ensuring that I doubt Your plan for me. What's more, my husband just vulnerably shared that he has been feeling financially burdened lately. I wonder now if Your Spirit is prodding me to assist my husband in providing an income for our family or if I am to remain steadfast in freely sharing the gospel with others. I know that You are not a God of confusion. Won't You please guide my next steps? I humbly ask this in Jesus' name.

Amen."

~GERMANY & RUSSIA~

December 20, 2016

Perfect Shepherd,

Several weeks ago, I followed Your lead and interviewed for a temporary position with a senior care agency. The interview went surprisingly well. Amazingly, the small business co-owners were a husband and wife team who had both come to America from different countries. The husband was from Germany, while the wife was from Russia. Instantly, I praised You for another opportunity to share You with the ends of the earth. *What an exciting adventure this will be!* I thought.

A few days before my first shift, You confirmed Your will through a song that played on my car radio. As I listened to the lyrics of "Light Your World" by the Newsboys, a stream of tears began to fall from my eyes. Soon after, those butterflies in my stomach began to flutter, once again confirming that I was on the correct path.

As I had never worked in senior care before, everything would be new to me: dentures, wheelchairs, gait belts, wigs, adult diapers, everything! Thus, before my first shift, I prayed fervently.

During the first hour of caring for my brand new 95-year-old client, I had to chuckle. A family friend of my new client, a man approximately my age, had stopped by for his weekly visit. In the man's hand was a small traditional Catholic communion host container. "Would you like to join us for communion?" the man humbly asked. "Once a week, I stop by, and we pray the LORD's Prayer together and receive communion. You are welcome to join us if you'd like," he added. Imagine my shock—I was getting paid to pray! I smiled throughout my entire shift. In my heart, I said a little prayer as well, "Thank You, LORD, for this sweet confirmation, for allowing me to continue to serve others for Your Kingdom, and for returning my soul to a place of rest and peace."

In Jesus' name. Amen.

March 2, 2017

Holy and Righteous Father,

In honor of the sacrifice of Your journey into the desert and in the hopes of drawing closer to You (Joel 2:12), for the next forty days of Lent, I've promised to fast and spend some extra quiet time alone in Your presence.

For Your glory, I've decided to devote all of my prayers toward my marriage. Even though I've married an imperfect man with an addiction, in my vows before You, I have agreed to love LeeRoy unconditionally. That's why I am praying that You will allow me to see my husband through Your eyes. Help me see LeeRoy as a precious gift from You, someone I should always treat with sensitivity, tenderness, and love. Father God, thank You for LeeRoy's life, his work, his provision, and for making our home a comforting, peaceful, and soft place for him to land. Please use me to relieve his loneliness, be his helper, greatest encourager, and closest earthly friend.

Father, may these heartfelt and humble prayers bring a song to Your heart and glory to Your Son Jesus' name in Whom I now pray.

Amen.

June 18, 2017

Dear Heavenly Father,

My joyful Salvation, today was a great day of ministry. Thank You for using me to reach the heart of a father.

We had arrived early to the Oakland A's vs. Yankee's game. Just as we took our seats, an adult man standing in the row directly behind us screamed out to his father, "Just push your way up there, Dad." Afterward, I watched as the man's father returned to his assigned seat with an unsigned ball and pen in hand, his head hung low. I immediately felt the warming presence of the Holy Spirit lay a burden of purpose on my heart. So, I leaned back and asked, "Would you like my son to ask for an autograph for you? We're missionaries, and he'd be glad to help you." The man quickly handed me the ball and pen.

Right away, Travis and I walked up to where Reggie Jackson was signing balls, caps, and shirts. "Excuse me," I softly said to the security guard who was telling everyone to get back, "Can my son get an autograph?" I asked. The man replied, "Sure," and directed us to the front. We remained there for a moment, anxiously waiting for Mr. Jackson to make his way back to where we stood. Sadly, the famous baseball player had moved on. Travis looked at me and said, "I don't want an autograph, Mom." Apparently, my young son had missed the purpose of our efforts. So, I explained to Travis that we were trying to share God's love with a stranger on Father's Day. Once he heard who the ball was for, Travis stood still, patiently waiting to be a vessel for Your glory.

Another twenty minutes went by, and Travis was ready to give up. Then all of a sudden, three Yankee Players began walking across the large grassy field towards us. As one very tall man drew closer, everyone started to scream his name "Aaron Judge!" By this time, Travis and I had made our way to the far-left corner of the fan signing area. We were now standing directly above a covered ramp. The three baseball players were headed straight for us! Suddenly, Aaron Judge reached up his hand and grabbed the baseball in Travis' hand. Without saying a word, he then signed the ball and handed it back to my little boy. Soon, all three baseball players had disappeared down the ramp. Travis' ball was the only autograph offered at that moment!

Travis and I returned to our seats. We both tried to grasp the significance of the moment. Then, Travis handed the stranger his brand new shiny autographed baseball. I leaned back to whisper in the man's ear, "This one's for you. Happy Father's Day from God!" The look on the man's face was priceless!

Also stunned, the man's adult son turned to me and said, "You know, my dad went around the house this morning repeating the same few words. He said, 'I want an autograph from Aaron Judge.' I am not even kidding!

He walked around the breakfast table, repeating the same thing many times. I can't believe he is now holding an autographed ball from Aaron Judge!"

Oh LORD, You are such a miraculous God. May this one moment in time be enough to encourage this man to surrender his heart to You. May he not only find hope in You but may he commit his life to the Father Who truly loves him.

In Jesus' name. Amen.

June 24, 2017

Light in the darkness,

Thank You for using me as Your ambassador in my own neighborhood.

I was still taking in our new environment's surroundings the day I first noticed the two young women walking past our home. Both women were using walking sticks to guide them down the street. Clearly, they were blind. That day, Your Spirit stirred within me, causing my heart to beat uncontrollably. So, I immediately ran outside to greet them. Right away, this pair of cheerful friends shared with me that they live nearby and often frequent the Starbucks up the street. We chatted for a while. Afterward, I wondered if perhaps You'd allow me to offer each of them the precious gift of Your Word.

Once we said our goodbyes, I returned inside our home to search online for Bibles written in Braille. Unbelievably, I immediately discovered an online ad that read, "Free set of Braille Bibles." My jaw hit the floor. A few days later, I met with a Stanford University Chaplain to receive these precious and timely gifts. I thought, *The next time I see the girls, I will offer them these Bibles along with a gift card to Starbucks. I can't wait!*

When the two girls next appeared, I ran outside of my home, carrying the giant bag of bulky binders, and excitedly offered my gift. That's when I learned that neither of the girls could read Braille. *Had I obtained this gift for nothing?* I instantly wondered.

A few days later, my neighbor's adult daughter was rummaging through her trunk at the same instant, I decided to take out our trash. "How's it going?" She called out. I shared with her my disappointment regarding the Braille Bibles. "Donna," she said. "My boyfriend is blind, and he can read in Braille. Can I give the Bibles to him?" My jaw dropped a second time. Eagerly, I ran inside our home and quickly returned with the Bibles.

There I was a few hours later, sharing my testimony with the woman's boyfriend. The man then shared with me the deep depression he had felt since he had lost his sight. "Most days, I don't even want to get out of bed. I've had three surgeries. I will never be able to see again," he said with sadness in his eyes.

I told the disheartened and weary man that there was still hope in Your Son, Jesus. "You are not alone," I said. "Anyone who sees their future as hopeless is blind. Although you are blind physically, the LORD will lead you along the right path if You let Him." (Isaiah 42:16) I added. He simply nodded his head in agreement and wiped his teary eyes. That was two and one-half years ago.

This past week Travis, now twelve years old, and I

learned how to play a worship song on a second-hand keyboard that I obtained not too long ago. At first, we weren't sure who the song was meant for. However, we had been singing this particular song in the car and thought that it might not be too challenging to learn how to play it on the keyboard.

Travis and I had just finished practicing the song when I noticed that my next-door neighbor's boyfriend was standing outside our neighbor's home. I went out to greet the man and humbly asked him, "Won't you please come inside my home for a moment? Travis and I have a gift for you." The man and his girlfriend came over right away.

Travis grabbed the keyboard and began to play the song while I sang,

> "Far be it from me to not believe
> Even when my eyes can't see
> And this mountain that's in front of me
> Will be thrown into the midst of the sea
>
> And through it all, through it all
> My eyes are on You.
> And through it all, through it all
> It is well…"

I could tell that the blind man was filled with raw emotions. Perhaps we all were. Soon, his tears had a domino effect. Once he started crying, one by one, everyone in the room began to wipe their eyes.

After the last note was played, I walked over to the man, grabbed my Bible, and read:

"And Jesus said, "For judgment, I have come into this world, that those who do not see may see, and that those who see may be made blind." (John 9:39)

"Do you know what that means?" I asked, still wiping away tears. The teary-eyed man shook his head, "no."

"Jesus was talking about giving us all faith to see," I said. Then, I told him that I'd be praying that he'd accept the Gospel message and be saved. In reply, the man humbly and sweetly thanked Travis and me for taking the time to do something so kind and personal for him.

Now, as I lay my head down to sleep, my heart fills with gratitude once again. Thank You, LORD, for that precious day back in October 2008 when You opened *my* eyes to see. And, thank You for allowing me to take this marvelous journey by Your side. What great comfort I have found in walking hand in hand with You, my Maker, Savior, and Friend!

Amen.

August 16, 2017

Perfect Restorer,

A few days ago, I began to feel ill. Instead of my usual high levels of energy, I felt beaten down, exhausted, and physically weak. *Could it be the flu?* I wondered. The sudden sickness came upon me so powerfully that I was forced to remain on the couch for three full days. I was feverish and nauseous, and I barely had the energy to lift my head. Strangely enough, no one around me was experiencing flu-like symptoms. In fact, no one even had a cold. What was going on?

As I lay motionless on the couch, I began to ponder the past few years of ministry. I recalled the many times I had suddenly fallen ill after experiencing a remarkable victory. *Oh LORD, why must the evil one be so relentlessly discouraging?* I wondered. Just then, a particular Scripture came to mind.

> "For we do not wrestle against flesh and
> blood, but against principalities, against
> powers, against the rulers of the darkness of
> this age, against spiritual *hosts* of wickedness
> in the heavenly *places*" (Ephesians 6:12).

As a result, I prayed and surrendered the situation to You. Afterward, I turned on the television to keep me company. As the hours passed, however, I became terribly bored. Although I felt physically afflicted, my spirits were still invigorated. So, I grabbed my laptop computer and plopped it upon my lap. Then I opened my Facebook page and typed the following. "The stomach flu has restricted me to crackers and the couch today. How can I pray for you?" For the next hour, I prayed intently over each prayer request. Unfortunately, with each tearful prayer I prayed, I felt my strength continue to diminish. Thus, I set my computer on the floor next to the couch and closed my eyes. Suddenly a sharp and overpowering odor grabbed my attention. I peeled open one eye and noticed our one-year-old male Chihuahua walking away from where I was lying. To my dismay, our small pooch had urinated directly onto my laptop. The atrocious smell began rousing my nausea even further. However, I was too physically weak to respond to the mess. At this point, I simply had to giggle. Darkness was trying its best to defeat me. Yet, I knew that Your hand was outstretched still and that You had the power to deliver me from Your enemy and mine.

Oh LORD, today I would like to thank You for Your mighty protection. Just as Your Word promises, what the enemy means for evil, You use for my good and Your glory (Genesis 50:20). In this case, You have used an attack by the enemy to force my body to slow down and refuel. For this, I am grateful! In fact, even with the inescapable stinky smell, still, I desire nothing more than to remain in Your presence, entirely overwhelmed by Your love. I love You too, LORD!

In Jesus' name. Amen.

~INDIA~

October 9, 2017

Divine Leader,

After having worked one full year in Senior Care, I felt Your Holy Spirit speak to my heart and say, "It is time to move on." Therefore, I submitted my two weeks' notice and began firmly walking toward the next call of ministry.

"What shall You have me do next?" I asked You one day during my morning devotional. A day or so later, You began using several measures to lead me. First, You caught my attention through movies about India. As I watched the movie about a five-year-old forced to survive alone in Kolkata, I wept. Afterward, I found myself engrossed in a film called "The Letters." Once again, I was wet with tears as I witnessed Mother Teresa's selfless service to India's "poorest of the poor."

Next, You used a radio station to guide me. While driving one day, I turned on my car radio—pure static. So, I tried to find another with clearer reception. While moving the dial back and forth, I discovered a radio station that I had never heard of before. Although I couldn't understand one word, I was sure that the woman on the radio was speaking one of India's languages.

Then, I received a phone call from a new mother of two twin infant girls. The woman had found my phone number online. "I need a mother's helper, someone to assist me with daily chores as I care for my two premature daughters. Would you be interested?" asked the woman politely. Then, she explained that her family was still adjusting to everyday life after spending the past few weeks in the Neonatal Intensive Care Unit. Instantly, my heart went out to her. However, considering how tired I was from juggling a part-time job and my family while keeping up our large rental and doing ministry, I almost turned her down. Then I remembered all that You had recently orchestrated in confirming Your will. So I accepted the position.

LORD, I am looking forward to my first day as a "mother's helper." My first day will be October 13, 2017. Thank You, God, for another opportunity to serve You!

Amen.

October 13, 2017

Joyful Salvation,

Today, I worked my first shift with the family from Tamil Nadu, India. It was inspiring to see such hope in the new parents' eyes and to hear those sweet infant cries. How invigorating it is to be around new life!

From the moment I walked through their front door, my senses were overwhelmed by colors, sounds, and aromas. I quickly noticed the brightly colored saris, the deliciously inviting fragrance of traditional Indian food, and what appeared to be a loving conversation in one of India's native tongues. My heart was warmed when I discovered that the infants' grandmother had traveled all the way from India to assist with her daughter's transition into motherhood.

The father of the children quickly introduced himself. "I'll show you what we are expecting from you," he said as he led me down the hall to the back bathroom. Along the way, we chitchatted in English about the differences between American life and the life the man left behind in southern India. It didn't take long before we built a rapport.

Once he demonstrated how to clean each baby bottle properly, he walked me back out to the kitchen area. "Here, you will wash the morning dishes. My mother-in-law cooks every meal from scratch," he explained.

Without a moment of hesitation, I put on a pair of protective gloves and began soaking the dirty dishes covered in stubborn stains. Then, I turned toward the grandmother. Using the only Hindi words I knew, I greeted her. The older woman smiled and stretched out her arms to offer me a warm hug. Then, she resumed her daily meal preparation.

I began scrubbing each bowl and plate with love and care. Since washing dishes is mostly a mindless task, I took a moment to contemplate my surroundings. I couldn't help but notice the Hindu statue upon the wall. Fresh incense was burning next to the idol, and a prayer mat rested below. Suddenly, Your Spirit whispered to my heart, "Don't pay attention to these objects. They are not the reason for your presence."

Meanwhile, the delicious scent of cinnamon, cardamom, and cloves caused my stomach to rumble. In my heart, I thanked You for allowing me to share Your redemptive message with people from all over the world while remaining in the safety of my own country. Surely all who find new life in Christ, from every tribe, language, people, and nation, will one day celebrate Your glory forever and ever (Revelation 5:9).

Oh LORD, I can't wait to see how You reveal Your providence!

Amen.

October 16, 2017

Missionary God,

Today was another rewarding day spent in the home of the family from India. Upon my arrival, I was greeted at the door by a loving hug. Amazingly, every family member seemed eager to learn more about You as they continually asked questions about my faith. Clearly, You had prepared their hearts for my arrival.

During my shift today, the young mother shared why her family had chosen me over all the other candidates. "It seemed strange to us that you were willing to work twice as long for only half the pay."

"You needed help, and I was available. If I am being honest, I would have worked for free," I replied with a gentle smile.

Toward the end of my shift, I suddenly felt fully equipped to declare the Gospel. Consequently, I began by sharing my testimony with the family. After I finished sharing my redemption story, I waited patiently for someone to translate what I had said to the grandmother. To my surprise, the woman had understood me completely. Not only that, but she was the most receptive of them all!

Tomorrow, I plan to bring a special flower arrangement for the grandmother and young mother as well as a paperback copy of my personal testimony for the new father. I cannot wait to share more about the hope I have found in You with each of these open hearts!

In Jesus' name. Amen.

October 18, 2017

⸻⸻∾ᴠᴠ∘σ⧵ᶿↃᐤᶻᶜↄ⧸ᴈ∘∘ᴠᴠ∾⸻⸻

Promised Hope,

Thank You for another great day of service! Once I arrived at my new place of employment, I got straight to work. I quickly washed all of the infant bottles before assuming my usual position at the kitchen sink—there were many pots and pans to scrub!

Feeling my normal chattiness coming on, I turned to the grandmother, who was busy cooking just a few feet away, and began a conversation. However, the minute I started to speak, she interrupted me and began to share what was in her heart. "I am reading your book," she softly said. "I like it very much." I was stunned! Yesterday, I had brought a copy of my testimony to their home, hoping that the father might read it. Never had I expected this lovely elderly woman, so well established in her own religion, to read what I had written about You. Truly, Your mysterious ways fill me with hope!

The family has asked me to stay on a little longer than initially intended while searching for a full-time nanny. I have graciously accepted.

Please, Father, flood me with Your Spirit so that I may be lovingly bold during the rest of my time with this family. Thank You for allowing me to share Your message of Salvation so they may come to know Christ as their Redeemer. Thank You for sprinkling my path with the surprising wonder of readied hearts!

In Jesus' name. Amen.

November 14, 2017

All-Powerful God,

Today I had a frightening encounter. For the first time in nine years, I believe that I faced something life-threatening, a moment that left me feeling completely powerless.

I had just dropped Travis off at school and was driving back home. It was a bright, sun-kissed morning, so I thought, *Maybe our little Chihuahua would like to go for a ride.* Since this puppy, named Charlie, is prone to car sickness, I rolled down the driver's side window. Charlie immediately crawled onto my lap. The fresh air blew in both of our faces as we drove back home. Pure joy!

When we approached a stoplight just a few blocks from our rental, my eyes locked with those of a stranger walking in our direction along the sidewalk nearby. Suddenly, I felt incredibly vulnerable and insecure. I couldn't explain my body's response to the sudden fear I felt. Yet, I instantly sensed something was wrong. As the man stared at me with blackened, malevolent eyes, an uncontrollable urge to flee had my feet restless. I sat there impatiently, waiting for the light to turn green while my mind struggled to make sense of the situation. For the first time since I began my journey with You, I felt I needed to avoid danger and serious physical harm. I needed to flee.

Not dropping his gaze, the tall and agitated man quickly picked up his pace in my direction and started yelling, "Don't you look at me! Don't you look at me!" He added a few curse words and continued pointing his finger at me. Not before long, he was standing directly across from where I sat in my car. I was utterly frightened! I held on tight to the puppy in my lap, hoping that evil wouldn't hurt us. The moment was so visceral, so palpable. I thought, *If only I could cower out of sight.* Trembling, I had all but forgotten that You are my fortress, protecting me from danger (Psalm 27:1).

I continued to hold on tight to Charlie, as a thought

repeated in my mind, *Please don't hurt my puppy*. Just as the man neared, I quickly jerked my head away, and miraculously, at the same time, the light turned green. With a massive sigh of relief, I began driving, and soon, we were back to safety again. I thanked You for allowing Charlie and me to leave the area unharmed.

Once we returned home, I began to pray, "Yahweh, Your Word says that You go before me and are my rear guard (Isaiah 52:12). You tell me to "Fear not, for I am with you; Be not dismayed, for I am your God. I will strengthen you, Yes, I will help you, I will uphold you with My righteous right hand '" (Isaiah 41:10).

With You guiding my every step, I know that I should not panic or be afraid of events beyond my control (Matthew 8:26). Nor should I fear sudden terror (Proverbs 3:25). Yet, today, I felt scared, and now, I am left wondering why.

For years, You've taught me not to fight evil in my own strength. You've shown me that You are faithful. And, You strengthened me and protected me from the evil one (2 Thessalonians 3:3). Consequently, I do not fear death (Psalm 23:4). Instead, I look forward to the day that I will one day be absent from the body and present with You (2 Corinthians 5:8).

Also, You say that I am Your creation (Isaiah 44:2), You fight for me (Exodus 14:13), I am loved (1 John 4:9), You are my helper (Hebrews 13:6), I am more valuable than the sparrows (Luke 12:7), and that Your presence is with me always (Deuteronomy 31:8). So why was I afraid?

Perhaps the events of today were simply meant to prompt my heart to remember Your mighty protection. LORD, thank You for guiding me in responding appropriately to the evils of this world. Thank You for helping me discern when to rebuke, when to pray, and when to flee to safety.

In Jesus' mighty name. Amen.

~ISRAEL~

November 15, 2018

Yahweh,

A dear friend of mine passed away this week. Such an unexpected loss! The unforeseen nature of his passing has given me much to ponder.

My friend, a Jew and Holocaust survivor, was in his mid-eighties. He was a well-mannered man and a genuine soul. We met four years ago in the Museum of the Holocaust in Los Angeles. One day, You had led me to this specific museum to demonstrate Your loving-kindness to Your Jewish people. Little did I know then that a deep, abiding friendship would blossom and that I would spend years pouring Your love into one particular Jewish man until the very end of his life.

One day, we arrived just in time to hear this special man's heartbreaking story. During that brief introduction, he spoke about his experience in surviving the devastating Holocaust. Then, he began to describe his deep abiding longing for his brother, the only other person in his immediate family to have survived the war.

Through tears, the tender, elderly man had shared how

much he missed his brother, who was currently living 7,600 miles away in Israel. With every tear that fell from his eyes, a heaviness set in my chest. I could barely wait for the man to stop talking so that I could approach him, hug him, and tell him how much You loved him.

When the man finished his speech, I walked as quickly as I could to his side and blurted out, "Baruch Hashem Adonai!" That day, my hair happened to be wrapped in a headscarf, and I was practicing speaking in Hebrew. Perhaps that is why he asked, "Are you Jewish?"

"No, we're Christians," I said, gesturing to Travis standing by my side. "We've come here today to tell you that God loves you very much," I added with a smile. Travis and I offered the gift we had brought for him and exchanged personal contact information before saying our goodbyes. As we left the building that day, I said out loud, "That man needs to see his brother one last time!"

When we returned to our trailer, I shared the details of our visit to the museum with my husband. "I want to sell our abundance in belongings to purchase a ticket to Israel for the sweet old man," I said. Surprisingly, LeeRoy was on board! "Don't touch my tools or my fishing poles. You can have the rest," he generously offered.

Week after week, I drove the five-hour round trip to our storage unit until every last item was sold. In the meantime, my friendship with the gentle and soft-spoken man flourished. We either called or emailed one another practically every week. Each time I spoke with the man, he shared what was in his hurting heart with me. In return, I spoke to him about Your love for him and the power of forgiveness.

On the last day of our storage unit sale, I added up the proceeds—$500! Unfortunately, the money I had raised didn't even cover half of one airline ticket. I needed a total of $2,300 for two round-trip tickets, one for my new friend and one for his wife. I felt so disappointed! Even so, I decided to offer the gift to my friend. So, I gathered up the profits and drove to the museum with Travis to see the man in person once again. This time, before approaching the museum entrance, I prayed, "Please, Lord, help me touch this gentle Jewish man's heart with this gift."

Then, we entered the museum and took our seats. A nearby high school had taken a field trip. As a result, a large number of attendees were waiting to hear the guest speaker that day. I was surprised when the man personally called out to me in the crowd. He had only seen me once before, but he looked me straight in the eye. Then, his eyes welled up as he yelled over the crowd, "Are you Donna?" I blushed and nodded. "Yes," I said and smiled. He nodded and smiled too, as if to say, "We can get started now."

After the man finished sharing his story, Travis and I walked over to where he stood. Excited, I handed him the special gift—a brand new soft leather wallet filled with cash. He opened the wallet and looked inside. "I know it's not enough," I started, "but please use this money for a ticket to see your brother." My friend's jaw dropped as he looked at me with surprise and delight. "I…I don't know what to say," he replied. "Did I tell you that my brother is in poor health and that I desperately want to visit him before he passes?" he added. We hugged. Afterward, I smiled sympathetically and said, "I will pray that God provides the rest of the money."

From his reaction, I knew right away that You had answered my prayer to touch his heart.

Over the next four years, the elderly man and I grew closer. A gentile and a Jew had been united in holy love. Our conversations mostly revolved around family, religious holidays, and You. He taught me what it meant to be Jewish, and I shared my knowledge about Your Son Jesus with him. My friend often surprised me when he'd welcome hearing about the Messiah.

On one occasion, I felt Your Spirit tug on my heart to reach out to my friend. For several hours that day, I listened to Christian songs sung in Hebrew by Messianic Jews. Since I wasn't sure what You might want me to say, I prayed a simple prayer first. Then, I sat down to type him an e-mail that included an internet link to the songs I had listened to. Not knowing the effect this act of obedience would have, I closed my eyes and pressed the send button. Imagine my surprise to read later his response, which said,

"Hi Donna,

Thank you so much for sending me that beautiful email. I must have spent at least an hour watching and listening to music. I did not know much about the Messianic Jews in Israel. I find it very interesting that there are so many in Israel, and I did not know anything about it. All the best and have great and enjoyable Thanksgiving."

On another occasion, my friend discovered a little book at a local garage sale that reminded him of me. He had innocently thought that the hymnal was a Christian Bible. "I don't know why I decided to pick the little book up. But once I saw what it was, I knew I had to buy it for you." He said during a phone call one day. He held on to that little book until he saw me in person.

I was offered this precious little gift upon my only visit to the man's home. He never knew because I never told him that singing was one of my favorite past times. In fact, I sang similar hymns to those in the little Methodist hymnal for years in a Catholic church choir!

Approximately one year after that home visit, my friend and his wife finally took that long-awaited trip to Israel. How could I have known that not only would his brother see him one last time, but soon, I too would have to say "goodbye" to my dear friend?

Last week, Travis and I were invited to attend my beloved friend's funeral. Since we weren't family, we politely stood behind all the chairs and watched the proceedings from afar. Amazingly, You had orchestrated that I stand next to one of the man's two adult sons. It wasn't long before we struck up a conversation. I shared that I was a Christian and a friend of his father's. The man looked shocked. Unexpectedly, he disclosed that he had read both the Old and New Testaments and had shared with his dad how he suspected that Jesus was the Messiah. I listened intently as the man's eyes welled with tears. "From that moment on, our relationship had become strained," he said, looking somewhat dejected. I hugged the man tightly and told him that You were with him. Then, we said our tearful goodbyes and headed home.

Since the cemetery was approximately six hours from our current rental, I had ample time to reflect upon the purpose of our friendship during the long drive home. I wasn't expecting that just minutes after entering the flow of freeway traffic, doubt would creep in. Soon my heart was filled with heaviness, and my shoulders were weighed down with discouragement. I knew that I had spoken about You as Creator, Almighty God and Father. *But, did I talk about Jesus enough?* I wondered. The thought that such a dear friend might spend eternity separated from You because I hadn't said or done everything I could to prevent it was too much to bear. Soon, my tear-filled eyes made it difficult to see the road ahead. Thus, I pulled up to the side of the highway and called my pastor's wife for prayer support. She immediately prayed, offering words of comfort and wisdom. Thankfully, her words were just what I needed to hear to dry my eyes and continue our long drive home.

By Your grace, Travis and I made it home safely. Unfortunately, the sinking feeling of regret wouldn't leave me alone. As hard as I tried, I couldn't stop the distressing thought that I hadn't led my friend in saying a prayer for his salvation. Therefore, I begged You to show me mercy and comfort me with Your grace.

Then, something extraordinary happened today that healed my heart and chased away those disturbing thoughts.

I was getting dressed up for my fifteenth wedding anniversary dinner when I received an unexpected call from a sister-in-Christ. She had a special gift for me and wanted to visit. "Are you busy now?" she asked, nearly bursting with excitement. "No, come on over," I replied, thrilled to see her. As she entered our home, she offered me a lovely gift bag. In the bag were two presents—a shawl and a perfumed bottle of frankincense. I smiled when I saw the word "JOY" printed across the front of the bottle.

Then, suddenly she shared, "I feel as though God wants me to pray for you right now."

"Of course," I humbly replied with a smile. I sat down on our old worn-out chair while my sweet sister-in-Christ knelt on the floor by my side. "I am learning to pray in tongues. I hope that doesn't scare you," she said with trepidation. For a moment, I felt unsure of what to do. Praying in tongues, to me, meant the ability to suddenly speak in a known, human language. Yet, I suspected that this was not what she meant. Therefore, I said a little prayer, "LORD, if her prayer is not from You, please protect my heart."

At that moment, my friend laid her hand upon my shoulder. Then, she nervously began to pray. Right away, I heard familiar words pouring from her heart. *Is she praying in Hebrew?* I wondered. As she prayed, my friend repeated a few of the same words several times. "Hashem... El Shoah..." she said. Then, in English, she said, "You did a good job. You are my servant, and I love you." Instantly, the burden I had been feeling mysteriously disappeared. I was at peace again and finally able to simply mourn the loss of my friend. Just like that, You turned a tragic moment in time into a glorious one!

I returned the heavenly gesture with the tightest hug I could muster. Then, I watched as my friend buckled her children into their car seats and drove away. Strangely, this friend had no idea about the inner turmoil I had been facing. In fact, I had never even spoken about my Jewish friend to her before. She was merely obedient to Your Holy Spirit, and in so doing, she showered my spirit with Your heavenly gift of peace.

As I walked back to our home, I grabbed the mail. There was a small "Thank you" card from my Jewish friend's wife among the thin paper solicitations. *You have impeccable timing, LORD!* I thought as I stepped back inside.

I began to apply my makeup again. All the while, I kept thinking about the meaning of the mysterious phrase, "El Shoah." So, I sat down at my computer and typed "El Shoah" into the search bar. Imagine my surprise when I read the description, "This phrase is often used to refer to the greatest modern tragedy to befall the Jewish people, the Holocaust!" I began to sob, and my knees became weak. Immediately, I bent down and placed my head upon the floor in utter surrender to You. I thanked You for the fantastic way in which You comforted me and removed my burden of anxiety. Once again, I was ready to face a day's march in the joy of Your strength. With You by my side, I felt equipped to take another step nearer to heaven.

In Jesus' name. Amen.

December 21, 2018

Good morning Jesus,

Today, I would like to thank You for how You make Your ways known to me.

A few days ago, the pages of my Bible landed upon Isaiah chapter six. Immediately, a few verses leaped off the page:

> "Then I said, "Lord, how long?"
> And He answered:
> "Until the cities are laid waste and without inhabitant,
> The houses are without a man,
> The land is utterly desolate,
> The LORD has removed men far away,
> And the forsaken places *are* many in the midst of the land.
> But yet a tenth *will be* in it,
> And will return and be for consuming,
> As a terebinth tree or as an oak,
> Whose stump *remains* when it is cut down.
> So the holy seed *shall be* its stump"
> (Isaiah 6:11–13).

As I delved further into these verses' meaning, my thoughts instantly turned toward a story that was all over the local news. Was my next task at hand? *Possibly*, I thought with a smile.

In a matter of hours, a raging fire had destroyed nearly

90 percent of the town of Paradise and some other hillside communities in Butte County—neighborhoods located approximately three hours from our current rental. The inferno had killed several people and plunged many of the residents of these cities into darkness. The more I thought about the survivors, the more I wondered if, perhaps, an act of kindness would confirm that, without a doubt, You are with each of them in their time of need.

Soon, I heard Your Spirit whisper to my heart once again, "A personalized note can calm a despairing soul." Consequently, I drove to the local Walmart to purchase a few boxes of greeting cards. In the store, an old familiar Christmas tune was playing over the loudspeaker. As I tearfully picked out Your heartfelt gift, I sang along, "The greatest gift they'll get this year is life…do they know it's Christmastime at all?"

Back at home, I sat at our kitchen table for hours, writing by hand exactly one hundred greeting cards. In the background, Christmas songs continued to play through our television speakers. At one point, You amazingly orchestrated that the same song I had heard in the bustling department store played a second time in my home. Sweet tears of confirmation overflowed as I wrote the message "God is with you" on each card.

Then, just as I began to develop a cramp in my hand, Travis suddenly appeared by my side and kissed my cheek. "What are you doing, Mom?" he asked. I shared the task at hand with my young son, who immediately pulled up a kitchen chair, sat down, and began to write his own message of hope. Pure joy filled my heart. Once again, my trusted and faithful companion helped me share You with this lost and hurting world. Hours went by until, finally, only two cards were left.

After adding the finishing touches to our final Christmas card, I decided to check in with the world over the internet. Once again, You confirmed Your plan for me, as the same tragic story suddenly popped up on my computer screen.

My eyes welled up as I read about a man and his wife combing through the rubble and remains of their burnt down home in the hopes of discovering their grandmother's Bible. Almost immediately, I found myself standing in another store line, this time to buy a Bible with the couple's names inscribed upon the cover.

Thank You, LORD, for sending us two by two into every city where You are about to go (Luke 10:3). I cannot wait to see how another story of Your love and grace unfolds!

In Jesus' name. Amen.

December 23, 2018

Suffering Savior,

Today, the pages of my Bible settled upon Isaiah, chapter forty. Immediately, the entire chapter enraptured my heart. "'Comfort, yes, comfort My people!' says your God…" (Isaiah 40:1).

As the hours passed, I began to dig a little deeper into one verse.

> "O Zion,
> You who bring good tidings,

Get up into the high mountain;
O Jerusalem,
You who bring good tidings,
Lift up your voice with strength,
Lift *it* up, be not afraid:
Say to the cities of Judah, 'Behold your God!'"(Isaiah 40:9).

As I pondered the words of this verse, my heart fluttered with excitement. Once again, Your Spirit was leading me in faith and holy obedience to some aching souls.

In the car, Travis and I held hands. "LORD, please help them know that even if they have nothing here on earth, they still have You, the best Christmas gift of all," my young son prayed passionately. Then, we began our long drive. Feeling encouraged, we sang along to a few of our Christmas favorites. Soon, the song called "Winter Snow" had me in tears.

We arrived in Paradise just as it began to rain. With no specific destination in mind, we stopped at the first building that was still standing amid the rubble. The smell of thick burning smoke immediately began to stream in through our car windows. Paradise had literally been reduced to ashes. The pungent smell lingered in the air as I cleared my throat to ask someone where the disaster relief building was. In her pajamas and wrapped in a blanket, one young woman directed us to a makeshift rescue center. "Many people are still living in their burned homes and cars," she said. I extended my arms to offer her a warm hug. Then Travis and I drove ahead to the place in town, distributing warm meals and water to residents. There, we were lovingly welcomed by a few members of a local Baptist church.

For about an hour, Travis and I sat among the residents and listened to their harrowing stories. The vacant building was cold and noisy. Suddenly, a playful black Labrador Retriever began brushing up against the side of my leg. His owner quickly introduced herself as one of the volunteers in charge of the shelter. In my usual fashion, I shared my personal testimony with the woman. In return, she carefully placed a special gift into the palm of Travis' hand—a bright blue glass marble with a picture of the world painted on it. "Go share the Gospel," she said to Travis with a cheerful smile. Then, Travis handed the marble to me. "Look, Mom," he said. As I glanced down at the precious gift, my heart filled with joyous delight and my eyes with warm tears. "*The Savior of the World*," I said under my breath.

Afterward, the woman shared a miraculous story with me. "A group of approximately thirty people was trying to outrun the fast-moving fire when they came upon a church building. They all ran inside. The pastor tried his best to keep them all calm and started to pray. Just then, a wall of fire surrounded the church. The people could see the hot and raging flames through the windows. The pastor continued to pray, and the fire passed by without causing any damage whatsoever. All of the people inside, as well as the building itself, survived!"

Her story was precisely the confirmation we needed. For the next few hours, Travis and I went door to door and car to car, handing out Christmas cards and offering hugs to those who were sinking in hopelessness, grief, and despair. Each gesture was received with a warm sense of gratitude, causing me to feel as though You were using Travis and me as a loving reminder of Your presence.

With approximately fifty cards left, we headed towards Magalia, an adjacent town, also devastated by the fire. We asked one of the residents where we could reach out to the most people in the least amount of time. A woman directed us to the local Rite Aid, one of the few drugstores that had survived the tragedy.

Travis and I stood just inside the door, handing out our remaining cards. The fifty remaining cards were in the hands of strangers within minutes. It was such a gratifying experience to see appreciative, comforted, and reassured looks upon their faces!

Back in the car, Travis and I received a few heavenly confirmations that we had, in fact, carried out Your will. First, a song I had never heard before called "Christmas Card" by Steven Curtis Chapman began to play on the radio. Misty eyed, I could barely see the road ahead as I listened to the words.

I had barely wiped away the tears when You confirmed Your presence once again in the form of two doves circling only a few feet above our car. The sweet birds then drew my attention to a rainbow spanning the entire sky above us. Right then, I quietly prayed, "Oh, LORD, being in Your presence and carrying out Your will is truly an overwhelming experience. Thank You for counting me worthy to serve You today. Amen."

While singing songs of praise to You, time passed by quickly, and soon we were home. Once inside our warm, dry, and cozy rental, I hung my head and said another little prayer, "Father God, Your Word says, 'The Lord is close to the brokenhearted and saves those who are crushed in spirit' (Psalm 34:18). I pray for all those crippled by a broken heart today as my own heart grieves with them. LORD, please help each person see Your mighty saving hand. Show each survivor just how You worked to save them. Assure their hearts that You have a future of hope waiting for them. If someone doesn't know You, please God, may the work of Your grace blossom in their heart. May this painful, scary, and dark situation become one that brings glory to Your name. I ask this in Your holy name, Jesus."

Amen.

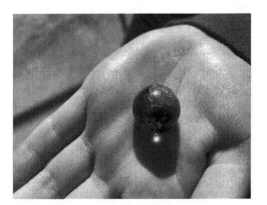

January 17, 2019

Alpha and Omega,

A few days ago, I followed Your Spirit to a nearby medical facility. There I met a woman in search of strength, hope, and peace.

It had been years since I made an appointment for a physical check-up. However, a few health issues had begun to hinder my ability to serve You. Therefore, I decided to call our military insurance carrier to request an appointment with a local doctor. While on the phone with our carrier, I took the occasion to share my testimony. Then I called the assigned doctor and made an appointment with a medical facility located only a few miles from where we live.

On the day of my appointment, I checked in at the busy reception desk. The receptionists were on overdrive and frantically attempting to assist all the patients. Despite this, I became deeply engrossed in conversation with a woman behind the counter, during which I shared a brief version of my testimony. "For 38 years, I called myself a Christian because I wore a cross, prayed to God and attended church regularly. Yet, I lied, gossiped, and judged others without mercy. One night I prayed, asking God to use my life to glorify Him, but I was ill-prepared for the response. I was arrested and charged with a felony! In deep and dark despair, I turned to Jesus Christ for help. He was there to save me as I sorrowfully repented for my past sinful behavior. Since then, Jesus has transformed my heart and blessed my life with unimaginable peace and joy."

While sharing my story of forgiveness with the woman, I somehow managed to capture the entire room's attention. Not only had the women behind the counter stopped moving, but the whole lobby had suddenly transformed from loud and bustling to dead silent. It seems everyone had stopped to hear about Your mighty power of forgiveness!

Afterward, I took a seat in the lobby and waited for my name to be called. Soon, a sweet and tender-sounding nurse appeared with a clipboard. "Donna, the doctor can see you now," she said.

Then, the young woman led me down the long hallway

to a private room. As we walked together, I shared my faith with her.

Sitting still upon the examining table, I waited quietly for the nurse to take my vitals. After she was finished taking my blood pressure, she began to share a story of her own. To my surprise, the woman openly and honestly narrated a scary experience that had recently occurred. She seemed genuinely frightened as she described what it was like to wrestle with a demon. Instantly, I felt intimidated. So, I took a deep breath and quietly said a prayer to You in my heart, "LORD, please take away this insecure feeling." Without delay, the still small voice of Your Spirit replied, "Be strong and courageous."

"I have no one to share this horrible experience with. Who would ever believe me?" she asked. Then, our eyes met. "I believe you," I replied compassionately. Before she could speak another word, I blurted out, "You are not alone. God is with you! And I will pray for you." A look of relief came over her face, and she became silent. Then, she left the room with a smile and a word of gratitude.

For the next few days, I prayed on my knees with tears pooling in my eyes. I cried out to You to help the kind and gentle nurse. "Please LORD, cover her with the warmth of Your love and give her peace that surpasses all understanding. Help her see the light of Your presence in moments when Satan comes on strong. Protect her from the evil one so she can be brave and courageous too. Lead her, restore her, and comfort her with the power of Your love."

In Jesus' name. Amen.

~MEXICO~

February 21, 2019

Incomparable Companion,

Thank You for our recent five-day mission trip to Tecate, Mexico. Thank You for deeming Travis and me worthy to follow at Your heels to bring good news to the poorest of the poor.

Seemingly overnight, my son became a teenager. As many teenagers in the states do, sadly, Travis began to take his comfortable life in America for granted. So, one night, while watching our favorite television show together, I said to my husband, "I want to take Travis out of the country. It's time. He's old enough now to share the Gospel with people in far off lands."

"As long as I don't have to pay for it," LeeRoy replied, on board with the idea. I smiled. After years of experiencing the miracles You wrought with money, I was confident that if this idea was Your will, money wouldn't be an issue. So, I applied to participate in an upcoming mission trip to Mexico with our current church body. Subsequently, each night, around the dinner table, I began to speak about the possibility of a mission trip to Mexico. I used my memory of past trips to the most impoverished regions on the Mexican border to guide my conversation. Soon, Travis's interest was sparked.

Then, one day at church, I took a leap of faith and wrote a check for the deposit. As I placed the envelope in the tithe box in the church's foyer, a voice called out to me. "You're going to Mexico!" a church member yelled from afar. It was official. Our application had been accepted. Little did I know that You were working behind the scenes!

A few weeks later, it was time to pay the final balance to cover the short-term mission trip's cost. I transferred the funds needed from Travis's savings account into my checking account and wrote another check. Then, I brought the envelope and the enclosed check with me to church the following Sunday.

After the service ended, I handed the envelope with the final payment to the mission trip coordinator. The woman simply smiled and extended her hand toward me, not to accept my payment but to offer me a little Post-it note. When I read the message, I began to cry. "Please tell Donna that her trip has been paid in full," the note read. Incredible!

I soon noticed that sweet hints of Your providence were scattered throughout the remote region where we would be serving You. I wondered if You were reminding me that You had gone before us, preparing the way.

First, You led our church members to a freshly constructed one-room cement building. Then, You assigned us the task of inviting all the neighbors to join us for a tamale lunch. The event was a first-time church fellowship for many in this neighborhood. It was challenging to organize it as it rained heavily for months upon the unpaved hills and roads. We had all dressed in our Sunday best, so for many of us, it took all that we had just to stay upright—squish, slip, squash, slide! For about an hour, our large group trudged through the mud calling out to the homeowners of each makeshift wooden shack.

We had wandered quite far from the little room of worship when I noticed that a young boy in the neighborhood was being bullied. Memories of Travis's recent painful bullying experience quickly filled my maternal heart with a wave of protective anger. I approached the group of boys who were picking on a child—he had notable scars on his head. "Cómo se llama (what is your name)?" I asked the tallest boy in the group in a stern voice. The boy instantly gave into his teenage immaturity and smugly replied, "Jose."

"And you?" I asked, looking at the next tallest. The second boy snickered and replied, "Jose," as any cowardly bully would. Then, another child in the same group looked straight at me and said, "We are all named Jose." They laughed. However, twenty plus years of working with troubled children had prepared me. "You are not going to believe this, but my name is Jose too!" I replied, in Spanish, with a smile. And just like that, the ice was broken. "Come on," I said in a softer tone, wrapping my arm around the shoulder of the boy closest to me. Soon, we had a following. The gang of boys, including the one picked on, was clomping through the mud by our side.

The boys were a nuisance during the first part of the fellowship, but the more we spoke about Your love for them, the more receptive they became. I watched as the boy "in charge" scooped up a little girl and tenderly held her on his lap.

After the church service ended, our large group, comprising thirty-two Americans, made our way to the top of a hill. We waited for our bus to arrive. At the top of the mountain, we were told that we had some time to spare. So, one group leader took a few of the children, including

Travis, back down the hill to a local convenience store, hoping to purchase some Mexican candy. I decided to stay behind and wait with the others.

Upon his return, Travis was smiling and filled with joy. "Guess what, Mom?" he said cheerfully. "We saw your name written on the wall down the hill!"

"Really?" I asked. "I'll bet it was misspelled." "Nope. It was spelled exactly the way you spell it," Travis said excitedly. I was just about to dismiss him when a few of the other adults in our group approached us and joined in on our conversation. "He's right. It was spelled D-o-n-n-a," our group leader said. "But how?" It was such an unlikely combination of letters in Spanish! For decades, I have always seen my name misspelled in Spanish, written as "Dana" or "Dona." So, the fact that it was spelled "Donna" was rather incredible. Plus, Donna isn't a common name even in English.

Our next day brought us a new task. Our group was going to construct an entire home, including three bedrooms, a loft, and an outhouse, for a young married couple with an infant—it was sure to be another day filled with wonder!

With no skills in hammering, I decided that I would spend the day painting. At first, Travis worked by my side. But after only an hour, my trusted partner wandered away. Travis joined a group of teenagers who were enjoying building wall frames.

I wasn't alone for very long, however. A woman about my age, who lived in a neighboring community, began to paint by my side. She spoke only Spanish but was relatively easy to understand. I tried my best to share my testimony with her in her native tongue. Her tearful eyes affirmed that she understood me. Then, she opened up and shared what was in her shattered heart. She spoke of the immeasurable pain that came from losing a child. Soon, we were both crying. "I will pray for God to heal your broken heart," I said in response. Then, I immediately began to pray to You to comfort her. Afterward, we resumed painting.

Almost immediately, however, our efforts were interrupted by the noise of a pickup truck engine's *rum-rum-rum*. I looked over my shoulder and noticed that a small truck was attempting to pull our school-sized bus, our only mode of transportation, out of four feet of sludge. I excused myself and walked over to our bus driver. It was clear that the endeavor of getting the bus out of the mud wasn't promising. "May I pray with you?" I asked politely in Spanish. "Sure," the driver replied as he hung his head.

Just then, two small children ran to my side. "What are we doing?" a little boy asked. "We are going to pray to God to help our bus driver," I replied. "Can we pray too?" he asked. I nodded. Then we all held hands and prayed, "Please, Father God, help our new friend. He needs You right now. I ask this in Jesus' name. Amen." The man thanked me while the two small children ran off to play. Then our bus driver began to remove the chains from the bus. As I returned to my painting duties, I wondered why he did this. Had he believed our prayer?

Almost immediately, a pungent smell began to drift around us. The stench was so putrid that the children started pulling their shirts over their noses. As I glanced up from my painting, I noticed a glorious sight. A large septic truck, equipped with an enormous flatbed, was backing toward the front of our bus. In a matter of minutes, the bus was pulled from the dirty mud and dragged to higher, firmer ground. Everyone on our team erupted in cheer and praise!

Just then, I felt Your Spirit tug on my heart to return to the bus driver's side. As I drew near, we made eye contact. The man shook his head from side to side as though he searched for an answer to where the truck came from. It seemed Your response to our prayer had opened the eyes of his heart. The bus driver and I now had a connection. Through his tears, the man described his longing for You. I tried my best to encourage him to seek You with all of his heart. We both talked about our families. That's when I was given another amazing gift. Miraculously, our bus driver had a daughter the same age as Travis, whose name was also Donna, spelled just like mine! Wow!

Soon, it was time to stop construction for the day—we had a schedule to keep. Our next job involved reaching out to impoverished families living in government housing known as "the projects." Our role was to share our testimonies and spread Your Word. So, we split into small groups and knocked on doors, inviting those in the area to join us for a few festivities in the park. The hours flew by quickly. I must admit that evangelizing came easily even when speaking in broken Spanish. I was in awe of each hurting soul that You brought to my side. Many hurting parents separated from their children by US immigration agents were begging me to pray that You might allow them to reunite with their children. How heartbreaking! I dug deep into my own heart and remembered the day that I was arrested and the resulting restraining order that prevented me from seeing or speaking to Travis. At the time, Travis was only three years old. My empathetic heart ached as I prayed for the broken hearts of these mothers and fathers.

The day wrapped up with another wonder. We had just begun our drive back to the ranch where we were staying when I heard a faint voice call out to me from the back of the bus. "Donna, did you know that I saw your name today?" our group leader asked. "You know how each person had to write their name on the sign-in sheet to receive a Bible at our last stop? Well, one person's name was Donna!" I began to tear up! Anticipating that her response might bring me to my knees, I asked her nervously, "Do you remember how she spelled her name?"

"D-o-n-n-a!" she replied. "Just like yours!" Immediately, I began to pray, "Precious Heavenly Father, majestic in glory, thank You for reminding me of Your loving presence in my life. Thank You for providing powerful signs, one after the other, affirming our mission trip! The fact that the improbable spelling of my name appeared not just once but three mighty times, much like the recurring pattern of the power of threes in the Bible, confirmed You are involved in every detail of my life. Thank You for using my time in Mexico to draw me even closer to You. Thank You for the gift of Your Holy Spirit, Who consistently guides me in where to go, what to do, and what to say to bring glory to Your name. Finally, thank You for allowing me to leave Mexico with a Spirit-filled story of my own.

In Jesus' name, I pray. Amen.

April 1, 2019

Heart Mender,

Betrayal can come as quite a shock, especially during times when we feel emotionally safe. Recently, I was reminded that church members are human too.

I had been part of the same Bible study group for years and was quite comfortable when a few church members unexpectedly did something hurtful. Sadly, I took the rejection personally. For about a week, I hid away at home. I tried to convince myself that organizing linen closets was as satisfying as being used by Your Holy Spirit to sow spiritual seeds in people's hearts. I told myself that I was spending some alone time just resting in Your love. "I'm casting all my anxiety on You, knowing that You care for me (1 Peter 5:7)," I repeated to myself. However, deep down, I longed to resume my role in bringing others to Your side. I desperately wanted to move forward in forgiveness. Perhaps that is why today, You sent an extraordinary summons straight to my doorstep to invite me back into the mission field.

Early in this morning, three floating red helium-filled balloons descended upon our home. Their vibrant color gleamed as they drifted above our sidewalk. I glanced out of our living room window just in time to catch the funny reaction from our neighbor's small dogs, who were curiously trying to make sense of the floating objects. Then, I returned to my chores, thinking, *Someone else is probably better suited to respond to this situation.*

Sometime later, the wind began to blow, causing the balloons to wrap around the tires of my husband's diesel truck. As the minutes passed, I became increasingly concerned. *They might do damage to his vehicle by getting caught in the wheels*, I thought. So, I decided to respond.

As I walked toward the red balloons, which had, by this time, completely settled on the ground, I noticed a white envelope attached to them. *A message. An invitation. Another task?* I wondered. I opened the card inside. But before I began to read what was written, I closed my eyes and said a little prayer, "Thank You, Father, for this opportunity. Please chase away my doubts and fears and fill me with new hope and courage to carry out Your will. In Jesus' name. Amen."

Afterward, I began to read. A hurting soul was mourning the loss of her father and was trying to reach out to him the only way she knew how. Each heartfelt word spoke of a love higher than any balloon could fly, a love deeper than any valley, a love between a father and a child created by You. My chest suddenly started hurting as I imagined the grieving woman's heartache. You had entrusted me with this stranger's broken heart, and I just knew that I had to respond. Perhaps You would use me to provide the one thing we all longed for so much after the loss of a loved one—healing.

Therefore, I conducted a quick search on the internet for the name inscribed on the card. *Will I find her?* I wondered. And, if I did, would I be brave enough to lead her home to her loving Heavenly Father? LORD, You've made me fearless in the past. Please give me courage again. I prayed. Amazingly, an address quickly popped up on my screen. So, I searched for directions to her home. Afterward, I filled a vase with a homemade flower arrangement. *Maybe a small gesture might soothe her aching heart.* I thought.

Afterward, I followed the driving directions to a quiet, classic American neighborhood. I parked my car, grabbed the greeting card and my homemade gift, and confidently walked through the white picket fence, straight to the doorstep of the stranger's home. Then, I rang the bell *ding-dang-dong* and waited. I could instantly hear the footsteps of a person moving slowly toward me. I could also hear the shaking sounds of a dog collar. Gradually, all the sounds from behind the door stopped. I rang the bell a second time, but there was still no reply. I started to wonder, *Is someone watching me from inside the house?* I smiled as I held my fragrant homemade bouquet of yellow-orange roses a little tighter. For a moment, I pondered how I had spent the past week isolated in my own home. *Perhaps the person behind this door is also trying to avoid further emotional pain by engaging with others*, I thought to myself.

A few more moments went by, and the only sound I could hear was coming from the sidewalk behind me. A man and a woman were strolling down the street together, chatting. It became apparent that it was time for me to walk away. Before leaving, I placed the bouquet on the doorstep beside the "Welcome" mat. Then, I left a message next to the flowers. On a small piece of paper covered with dainty flowers, I wrote, "Hello. My name is Donna Young, and I am looking for a woman named _____. If you know her, could you please contact me at…"

When I returned to my car, I found myself thinking about the women who had crushed my spirit at church. Instantly, I felt Your Spirit flood my heart with forgiveness and love as I remembered that Christ's atonement ensures that someday every tear will be wiped away.

Feeling strong once again, I knew what I had to do. I needed to pray for the women who had mistreated me. Then, I needed to forgive them and bless them in some sweet, personal way. And, by Your grace, that is just what I did!

Amen.

June 25, 2019

I AM,

Of late, I have been praying fervently for my young son's heart. As a teenager, Travis seems to be losing his enthusiasm for sharing Your Word with others. It appears to me that my son is going through that independent-yet-dependent stage. And, like me, is prone to wander. Thus, I've been praying that Travis will find his way back to Your side (Jeremiah 10:23).

"Perhaps he has heard my voice enough, LORD," I said during one morning's devotional. "Won't You please help me in restoring my son's excitement in walking this path with You?" A few days later, I walked into Travis's room and noticed that his Bible was resting on his lap. It had been a while since Travis had held his Bible without my prodding. "Are you okay, son?" I asked. "Yes," Travis replied with a confused expression. Silence filled the space between us. Curious, I probed further. "What happened?" "I just received a call from two of my classmates. They were together when they decided to call me. I could hear them both speaking through their phone's speaker. One asked for prayer on behalf of the other. At first, I thought it was a joke, because, well, you know how these two friends have treated me in the past. But when one earnestly asked for me to pray for the other, I immediately replied, 'Sure.' Then, I placed my Bible on my lap and began to pray. When I was finished praying, my friend thanked me sincerely. Then, they both said 'goodbye' and ended our call."

Travis wasn't aware of my prayer for him. I smiled, assuming that this divine intervention was Your answer to my prayers. As I began to walk away, I paused for a moment, turned back around, and said, "Good job, Son."

Today, Travis shared an even more meaningful experience with me. In one crystal clear moment, Travis had heard You speaking to him. It was early this morning, just after he had woken up. My son plopped himself down upon the couch and called out, "Mom? I think God spoke to me last night." Then, he paused. Stillness filled the room. I had to bite my tongue to allow him to explain more about his experience. "God's voice was very deep!" he added. Then, he said something exciting. "Do you know what He said?" I remained silent. "He said, 'Thank you, Travis, for being my son.' It made me feel good, Mom. I felt a little fear. But, it was the right kind of fear, you know, the kind that encourages you to respect God."

I instantly wondered, *Is this true? Did You, our God most High, utter Your voice to my youngest son?* (Psalm 18:13–15). My heart was filled with gratitude as I began to share with Travis about my own experience of hearing Your voice. "Travis, I too, have heard God speak. He seems to do this in many ways. God usually speaks to me through Scripture. But sometimes, God speaks in other ways as well—through dreams, a song, or Bible verse remembered at the right moment. God also speaks to me through a whisper to my heart. On a few particular occasions, when He chose to speak to me using His mighty voice, the sound was unmistakable! The voice of our God is low in pitch and booming. A sound that somehow vibrates throughout your body all at once," I shared.

Later, I opened my Women's Study Bible. My heart skipped a beat when I noticed that the pages had landed upon the Gospel of John Chapter Ten.

> "To him the doorkeeper opens, and the sheep hear his voice; and he calls his own sheep by name and leads them out. And when he brings out his own sheep, he goes before them; and the sheep follow him, for they know his voice." (John 10:3–4).

Sweet confirmation! In another surprising way, You confirmed that You were personally shepherding Travis and me. Thank You, Father, for being such a mighty God and for knowing and loving us both so intimately. Thank You for making both of us sensitive to Your voice within, a voice that always sounds like *LOVE*."

Amen.

~*CHINA*~

June 30, 2019

Majestic and Holy LORD,

Today, I humbly approach Your throne to inquire about another responsibility of my pilgrim journey. Lately, my calling to evangelize has included a prophetic insight that makes me feel tremendously ill-equipped. Even so, I am trying my best to be obedient.

Over the years, I've treasured the Old Testament prophets. Somehow, You sovereignly spoke through the words of ordinary men and proved that You are still active and in control of our lives. Amazing! Never could I have imagined that one day, You'd use *my* words to move beyond evangelism, disclose secret sins, predict future events, and bring comfort to the body of Christ (1 Corinthians 14:3-4, 24-25).

The first time I felt led by Your Spirit to speak prophetically of the future was in 2011 while I was still employed as a social worker. One day, I heard myself caution my employer against taking Your name in vain. "Repent or remove God's name from every business card, sign, and letterhead. If you don't, there will be no trace of this business within five years," I said. Soon afterward, I followed Your lead and resigned from my position with that employer.

A few years later, I curiously conducted an internet search for that particular company name. Incredibly, the business had utterly ceased to exist! In fact, only a few non-traceable internet links remained to indicate its presence in this world at all. Oh, the fate that awaits those who ignore God's warnings!

It wasn't until several years later that I experienced another predictive occurrence. This time, You had brought me to the side of a woman who was going through a season of defeat and hopelessness.

Travis and I had just begun to attend a new church in the area. To make fellowship with like-minded believers, I joined the woman's Bible study program. For a while, I bounced around between study groups. Then one day, You orchestrated that I join one specific small study group. Right away, I felt Your Spirit lead me to share my testimony with one particular woman. She was around my age and had also been raised in the Catholic religion. Thus, we made an instant connection. For several months, we sat across the table from one another while we studied Your Word. Then one day, she was absent. Wondering if she was okay, I quickly sent my new friend a text message. Sadly, the woman shared that she had been diagnosed with cancer. I immediately began to pray for complete healing.

A week or two later, my new friend attended Sunday morning service. I noticed her right away in the lobby. I teared up as she described the paralyzing sadness and fear she was feeling over her diagnosis. While she spoke, I gazed into her weepy eyes. I prayed, "Please God, allow my words to resonate with her." Then, when she finished speaking, I laid my hand upon her shoulder and uttered a few words with deep humility and concern. Even I felt shocked at what had been said. "You will not need chemotherapy," I said firmly. As the powerful and transformative message of hope flowed from my lips, the rest of me froze with fear. What if these words are not from You? I questioned. I hadn't read anything in Scripture preparing me for the moment. I hadn't felt Your Spirit stirring my heart. Oh LORD, what if I'm wrong?

Afterward, the woman had surgery to remove the cancerous tumor. Meanwhile, You continued to use me to accompany her on her road to healing. Then one day, the woman shared some puzzling news. "I went to my follow up doctor's visit." She said. "My doctor tells me that I will need to undergo chemotherapy after all." I exhaled noisily. Then, I looked straight into her eyes. Suddenly, my head began to shake from side to side slowly.

"No?" She asked, looking perplexed. My head continued to move back and forth. "Okay, Donna." She said with a smile. "I am going to hold you to that." Then, she walked away with an ear-to-ear grin.

As I took my seat with the rest of the congregation, my heart filled with reservation and uncertainty. Knowing that when I trust You, I don't need to understand, I immediately began to pray,

"Please, Father, don't allow Your Word to fall to the ground. (1 Samuel 3:19) Assure me that this hope-filled prophetic message was from You."

For the next few days, I felt unsettled. So, I prayed

without ceasing. I couldn't shake the feeling that I needed to speak with the woman again. So, I sent her another text message and asked if she needed anything. The woman quickly responded. "I had another follow-up meeting with my doctor. I couldn't help but think of you when the doctor said, "You won't need chemotherapy after all." *Praise God!* I thought as I sobbed as I fell to my knees.

These two instances were mind-boggling, but they weren't the only ones. Recently, I found myself in the middle of a short conversation with the landlord of our brand-new rental home. During our brief encounter, You once again used my words to speak comfort directly to a woman's heart.

The woman and I had only met briefly to sign the rental agreement. I quickly shared that I was a Christian Evangelist. She surprised me when she replied, "I'm a brand new Christian!" I offered to walk her to her car. As we walked along, I thought, *There go my hands sweating again.* Clearly, You were prodding me to share my testimony with the stranger. Thus, I obeyed.

By the time I finished my story, her face was filled with shock and amazement. Perhaps she felt comfortable with me because she immediately began to share her deepest fears. She spoke about her baby, who had been born prematurely. Her infant was currently struggling to hang on to life in the hospital. Without reservation or considering the consequences of my words, I blurted out, "Your child will live." Upon hearing these words, the sweet and soft-spoken woman looked at me with even more shock. She hugged me tightly. Afterward, she silently walked to her car and drove away.

As I walked back into our new home, my mind was

filled with anxiety and worry. *What if I am wrong? Did I just offer false hope to a brand-new Christian?* I wondered. *If I spoke out of turn, what will happen to her faith if her son doesn't live?* But just before my mind was flooded with dread, a calm came over me, and my heart was filled with peace. Another thought came to mind. *What if Your Holy Spirit was using my words to console and comfort this new believer?*

Oh LORD, please work in a powerful way to heal this woman's child, not only to nurture her faith but also to illuminate her life with your glory and mercy.

In Jesus' name. Amen.

~*KOREA & CAMBODIA*~

July 12, 2019

Immanuel,

Thank You for allowing me to glimpse the far-off country called Korea. Thank You for how You consistently use me to reveal Your loving heart to others.

I had heard about the owners of our landscape company long before I met them. Our landlord had nothing but positive things to say about the sweet Korean couple they had hired to manage our rental back and front lawns.

As part of our lease, we had agreed to pay for the general grounds keeping of our home. This meant that we would have to pay a hefty sum to a landscape company to have two men mow and edge our lawn. At times, the two gardeners who cared for our yard raced to get their job done, causing minor damage to the sprinkler system. It fell upon me to contact the owners directly for assistance at such times.

The couple responded quickly to each call. Since the husband spoke very little English, the wife was usually the one to return my call. Afterward, the husband would promptly arrive at our home and quickly resolve the issue. He was a hard-working, pleasant, and joyful man who always greeted me with a smile.

After a few visits, I began to anticipate the man's arrival. It was always the same routine. While he parked his truck out front, I'd secure our dogs inside. I'd then offer simple greetings in Korean as we met at the area in the yard that needed his attention. This went on for years.

Then, one day, we received a sixty-day notice to vacate. The owner of our home had passed away, and the house was now up for sale. While I felt that You were leading us to greener pastures, I also began to feel as though I hadn't done enough to share the Gospel with the Korean couple. I had never directly told them about Your ability to forgive their sins. So, I rested my head on the floor and prayed, "LORD, won't You please provide a way for me to share Your Word with this couple? I want to say goodbye, memorably."

A few hours went by, and I felt a sudden desire to browse through the free internet classified ads. While browsing, I came across an advertisement for a brand-new free Christian Bible translated into the Korean language. Without a moment of hesitation, I called the number listed in the ad and spoke with the owner of the Bible. I immediately felt at ease in sharing my testimony with the man. "You have an amazing testimony. When you come to visit, you should speak with my wife, who also has a remarkable story to tell," he said. Delighted, I made an appointment.

On the day of our meeting, the man gave me a quick tour of their homegrown backyard garden, where the couple spent much of their time. Then, he offered me a cold beverage and a seat at the counter height table in their shady stoop. The man's wife joined me and began to share her very personal harrowing story. "In 1975, at the age of eleven," she began, "my younger brother and I were being raised by our great aunt in the city limits of Battambang, then the second-largest city in Cambodia. Do you know much about Cambodia?" she asked.

I shook my head. "Okay, well, back then," she continued, "we were under the control of Cambodia's communist regime, the Khmer Rouge. People were either executed as enemies of the regime or died from starvation, disease, and overwork. When the Khmer Rouge took control, my entire life turned upside down. My family was already divided due to our own issues, and now we were forced into labor camps. I barely survived."

I choked back tears as I listened to the story of her remarkable escape, trying my best to be in the moment with her. The woman's story conjured up memories of the horrific accounts I had heard while ministering to Jewish Holocaust survivors not so long ago. At one point, tears of mercy spilled over from the corner of my eyes. In both tragedies, human beings, Your creation, had experienced so much evil, pain, and death!

When the woman finished sharing her story, she looked at me with sincerity in her eyes and said, "I've spent my entire life on a long quest to find God. Is God even real?"

I could feel my heart begin to race, and without hesitation, I placed my hand upon her shoulder and replied, "That is the very same question I asked the night I was in a jail cell eleven years ago. My life had turned completely upside down, and I desperately needed to know if God was real. So, I cried out to Him and asked, 'Are you even real, God?' Amazingly, God responded! He even sent someone to my side to confirm His presence. Perhaps He is now using me to confirm His presence in your life?" We both sat there, completely still, for a while.

After several minutes, I broke the silence. "I brought you some fresh heads of cabbage," I said. "I wanted to offer you a gift in exchange for the Bible." Her husband must have overheard our conversation because he immediately ran to get the plastic bag filled with carefully picked and blemish-free cabbage heads. "Your husband told me that you like to use cabbage for your favorite homemade Cambodian soup," I said. The woman offered me a hug. While she went to retrieve the special Korean Bible, her husband shared more of his own incredible story with me. "I am a writer," he said, handing me a copy of his work.

Afterward, we said our goodbyes. Before I drove away, I took a moment to observe the Korean Bible resting on the passenger seat beside me. I picked up Your Word and gently held You in my hands. While the beautiful leather cover, gold leaf page edges, and intricate writing filled my heart with Your goodness and grace, I wondered if the owners of our landscape company would give thanks to You upon receiving the gift. Then, I thought about the night You first saved me, and I became so overwhelmed that I began to weep quietly. Not only had You poured out Your Holy

Spirit to save me but also, somehow, qualified me as Your instrument of peace. It seems that to reach out to a broken world, *we* need to be broken first. Thank You, God, for pleading through me to heal the broken hearts of this world.

Amen.

December 26, 2019

Mighty Deliverer,

Recently, my circumstances led me to feel poor in spirit. For several days straight, I desperately cried out to You, praying for relief. Usually, after I pray this type of prayer, I feel Your strength move me forward. However, this time, the awful feeling of anguish and grief remained. I wondered what was going on.

The feeling of heaviness and unbreakable sadness had crept in one day, seemingly out of the blue. One morning, I woke up feeling as though I were under a weighted blanket. My heart, mind, and soul felt weak and numb. Suddenly, I felt smothered and trapped by gloom. For the next few days, I woke each morning to a dark and cheerless feeling. I tried to lift the weight off me, but no amount of prayer or Scripture seemed to lift the heaviness.

I had just begun the process of publishing my second book, and everything seemed to be going smoothly. My youngest son was attending a new high school and making a few new encouraging Christian friends. LeeRoy also seemed to be doing well. Each day, he returned home from work with a satisfied look upon his face. At night, we would all gather around the dinner table to enjoy a meal together and say a prayer of thanks. By all appearances, our home was peaceful. *So, what is the cause of this deep, alarming, and troubling feeling?* I wondered.

One day, as I stood in a grocery aisle, a simple decision caused tears to flow. "What cereal would bring the most joy to my husband?" I asked myself, feeling completely overwhelmed. While wiping away tears, I began to scold myself. "This is wrong. I should be experiencing the joy of the LORD," I said under my breath as I searched my purse for a tissue to wipe my nose.

Feeling discouraged, I turned to You for strength. *Perhaps I need to repent for something?* I thought. Back at home, I opened Your Word, but not even Your Word could bring me comfort. On the contrary, that heavy blanket over me seemed to press down even harder. If this was an attempt by Satan to kill my spirit and destroy my confidence, it was working.

Days of unbearable sadness turned into weeks. Such heaviness! I found myself continually asking You, "Why are You allowing this mysterious deep, dark, and all-consuming depression to cover me, LORD?" (Mark 14:34). Then, I forced myself to go about my daily tasks, keeping a clump of tissues in my pockets at all times as my soul gasped for peace.

For the first time in eleven years, I took no delight in ministering to others. The sense of fulfillment in doing Your will had all but disappeared. Melancholy and anger had somehow replaced my usual deep compassion. If it weren't for Your steady hand lifting me, I wouldn't have been able to get out of bed each day (Ezekiel 3:14). Soon, others began to notice that the usual spring in my step had all but disappeared.

One day, feeling exceptionally low, I decided to reach out to a sister-in-Christ for prayer support. My faithful friend dropped everything to answer my phone call and prayed for me right then and there. During the conversation, she suggested that my low mood could be associated with a lack of sunlight. Thus, I spent the next day outdoors gardening, hoping that it was just a vitamin D deficiency or an uncomfortable side effect of being a woman in her late forties. Sadly, I woke up the next day with the same utter despair.

Not before long, it was Christmastime. What was usually the second most joyous time of the year, second only to Resurrection Sunday, now felt empty and meaningless. The only Christmas special I could relate to was "It's a Wonderful Life." For the first time since surrendering my heart to You, I felt as hopeless as the desperate George Bailey in need of a compelling reason not to commit suicide. What's worse, I could suddenly identify with the Apostle Paul, who felt conflicted between having a desire to depart and be with You and to remain here on earth to be an available, loving example for the people in his life (Philippians 1:23–24).

As a last resort, I prayed once again, "LORD, please restore to me the joy of Your salvation and uphold me by Your generous Spirit" (Psalm 51:12). Almost immediately, I felt a strong desire to speak to my husband and share, with complete vulnerability, what I had been experiencing. So, I walked over to him and said, "Honey, I don't know what is happening to me. I can't shake this feeling of depression. I am sad all the time. Even while grocery shopping, I struggle to fight back the tears. If I emerge from the sadness for even one moment, all I feel is rage—not anger, rage! Then, in a split second, I go back to feeling sad again. It's horrible! If a person could die from sadness alone, I suppose this intensely painful feeling would be enough." Right then, LeeRoy embraced me. Never before had my husband hugged me so tightly!

Then, amazingly, a few days before Christmas day, as mysteriously as this debilitating sadness had come over me, it disappeared. You lifted that horrible cloud of sorrow from my head and flooded my heart with the joy of the season!

In the weeks that followed, You spared no time in leading me straight to three women around my age who had recently lost their adult sons to suicide. As I had felt the darkness that can overcome a soul, I was able to convey Your care and concern for those suffering from this type of tormenting sadness (Acts 4:32). I now believe that You had allowed me to experience depression to get under and help lift the heavy load of others suffering the same type of devastating sadness.

Today, I thanked You, LORD, for allowing me to help others hold up under the weight of unbearable sorrow. I thanked You for paving the way for me to touch more hearts with the power of the Gospel. Once again, my feet are joyfully walking forward toward those You place in my path.

In Jesus' name. Amen.

"My flesh and my heart fail; *But* God *is* the strength of my heart and my portion forever." (Psalm 73:26).

~RUSSIA~

January 29, 2020

Son of Man,

Recently, I drew closer to You to hear Your voice on a matter close to my heart. Over the years, I had somehow allowed my heart to fill with disbelief regarding Your promise to save my household (Acts 16:31). Consequently, I prayed,

Abba Father, please help me to settle down and patiently wait for Your Spirit to work in the hearts of those who have not yet surrendered to You. Renew my faith and give me unfailing certainty that what You have promised to do You will do (Romans 4:21). I want so much to believe You when You whisper to my heart, "I have a much greater plan. Trust me!" A few days later, You comforted me in a very unexpected way.

LeeRoy and I had just pulled our truck into the driveway after a short trip to pick up a free used treadmill. That's when I noticed some strange activity occurring in a house across the street. A few days prior, the "FOR SALE" sign from the neighbor's lawn had been removed. *That house sold quickly*, I thought to myself, but a quick sale of a residence in our new neighborhood wasn't unheard of.

What set this sale apart were the two white commercial vans with blacked-out windows that had pulled into the driveway just one day after the sign was removed from the lawn. I watched, intrigued, as two men unloaded large black industrial-sized garbage bags into the empty garage.

Playfully, I asked my husband, "Who moves into a new home with trash bags and white vans?" I must have watched too many documentaries about Russian spies in recent weeks because I jokingly added, "Maybe they are Russian spies!"

Then, today, while sweeping the leaves that had fallen in front of our home, I noticed the same two men across the street. This time, they were shuffling those garbage bags into the house. It was an exceptionally warm day outside, so I thought, *Maybe they are moving in and could use some water.* I decided to walk across the street, broom in hand, to welcome our new neighbors to the neighborhood.

With two cold bottles of water in one hand and the broom in the other, I called out, "Hello," from the curb in front of their home. The first man responded, "Hello," in a strong Russian accent. He didn't seem to speak much English. So, I spoke the few words I knew in Russian. Almost immediately, the second man joined our conversation. He, too, spoke with a Russian accent but was fluent in English. "There's been a misunderstanding," he said with a smile. "We are not moving in. We are only here to install the air-conditioning unit." This was enough to break the ice. Before I knew it, I was sharing my testimony with the two men. While the first man walked away, the man who spoke English listened quietly. Immediately after I finished speaking, the man began to share about his faith in You. Imagine my surprise when he mentioned that he also attends a Calvary Chapel Church!

Not before long, the two of us were laughing and encouraging one another. We praised Your Son for all that He had done for us. I shared my prayer from a few days ago. Right then and there, the man grabbed my hand and began to pray for my entire family. He prayed that You might create a situation that would allow each unsaved member of my family to surrender their heart to You. He also prayed that You would give me the grace to endure. Finally, he prayed that You would be glorified. As the man prayed, I found myself searching my memory for a few words in Russian that would signify agreement with his prayer. *Da Bog*, which means "Yes, God," came to mind. I thanked the man for allowing the Holy Spirit to work through him to encourage my heart. Afterward, I walked back to our side of the street, in awe of You.

As I entered my home, I pondered over the stranger's mighty prayer. Suddenly, I felt inspired to pray to You again, "Who am I, O Lord God? And what is my house, that You have brought me this far? Now, therefore, let it please You to bless the house of Your servant, that it may continue before You forever" (2 Samuel 7:18, 29).

Then, throughout the day, I continued my prayer to You. I prayed, "Oh LORD, please find it in Your heart to accept my Russian brother-in-Christ's prayer to save my family members. I know that You are the Lord, the God of all flesh and that there isn't anything too hard for You. I do believe; help me overcome my unbelief (Mark 9:24). Place Your fear in all of our hearts so that we together may worship You. Please LORD, rejoice over my loved ones with all of Your heart and with all Your soul. I want so much for Your glory to shine!

In Jesus' name. Amen."

April 24, 2020

Sovereign God,

Just as a deadly virus struck the area, I received a warm email from a woman who lives in an adjacent community. This particular woman had previously donated several gift items to me after closing her large department store doors. Once again, she offered me an opportunity to pick up an entire driveway filled with a large assortment of items— home décor, ornaments, greeting cards, and personalized gifts. Knowing that every good and perfect gift comes from You, I jumped at the opportunity. Initially, I wasn't sure who these items were meant for, but I felt confident that Your Spirit would lead me to the correct recipient.

The pandemic had impaired our ability to connect with one another in person. Now, the only form of contact was through a text message, a phone call, or a silent wave through a building's glass window.

For weeks, I watched as the news reported a rising number of deaths. Meanwhile, doctors and nurses tirelessly cared for overcrowded emergency rooms. *Perhaps these gift items were meant to demonstrate Your concern for those caring for others on the front line*, I thought. Over the next several days, I carefully packed the truckload of items into individual gift bags. By the time I had finished, bundles of presents were sprawled all over our living room. Next, I excitedly began calling local hospitals. However, with each call, I received the same reply, "Thank you, but we cannot accept anything from the public at this time."

My husband seemed overwhelmed by the outpouring

of Your generosity. He withdrew his emotions and simply remained silent. But after a few days, LeeRoy's anxiety regarding the numerous bags began to spill over onto me. So, I texted my pastor's wife back home and requested prayer support. "Please pray for God to show me where these gift bags should go," I said. "I believe these items were supposed to go to nurses at a nearby hospital, but the hospitals sweetly refused them. Now I am not sure of God's plan."

My dear friend simply replied, "You made them out of obedience. God will lead you to where they should go. I will pray." After a few minutes, I felt a strong desire to turn the news back on. A nearby assisted living center had experienced a high number of deaths, and many staff members had tested positive for the virus. My cheeks were soon wet with tears. The family members of the deceased, as well as the staff members, were all emotionally devastated! Suddenly, I felt the warmth of Your Spirit confirm Your will in my heart.

So, today, Travis and I woke up early and drove to the center. I didn't contact anyone before our arrival; we just showed up. Before we could even pull into the driveway, we were greeted by a man walking on the street in hospital scrubs. "Do you need any help?" he asked. I shared my intentions to bless the staff with Your thoughtful gifts. "Drive around to the back of the building. You can unload your gifts there," he said politely.

We did as instructed. The staff was now patiently waiting in the driveway. For over twenty minutes, Travis and I unloaded our car. All the while, I spoke about Your goodness. Too soon, the time came for us to say our goodbyes. The director of the facility was standing on the curb, looking tearful. I quietly approached her and stood by her side. She was at a loss for words. I said, "God is with you," as I handed her a greeting card I had made especially for her. The woman clasped her hands and bowed to me. "Never me," I said. "God alone is worthy of praise and honor." The woman smiled and straightened back up.

Even though I missed the excitement of watching each person's reaction to their presents, I still felt fulfilled in carrying out Your will. Thank You, LORD, for sending me as Your ambassador today.

Amen.

~AFRICA~

May 30, 2020

Sovereign LORD,

My heart was still tender when You first introduced me to the continent called Africa. One day, a television commercial aired in between the cartoons I had been watching. The commercial featured candid images of children who were surviving on only dollars a day. Instantly, I was drawn to the continent and filled with Your love for the least of them.

As I grew in stature, that precious childhood calling continued to nudge at my heart. In my early teenage years, I shared my firm conviction with my mother and new stepfather. "Someday, I'm going to become a Missionary," I announced.

Then, after years of fighting that same urgent and undeniable desire to go to Africa, at last on July 28, 2000, at age 29, You orchestrated a short-term mission trip that allowed me to experience Africa firsthand. Africa turned out to be even more of a surprise than I ever could have imagined. Looking back now, I can see Your mighty plan.

I had only been in Mombasa a short time before You sent a child from an adjacent village to reach my heart. The small child asked me if I'd take a walk with her. I immediately said, "Yes." As we walked along the unpaved clay dirt road towards her home, the sweet child proudly spoke about her life. A smile remained upon her cheeks the entire time. Then, as we neared her clay dirt hut, we stopped for a moment. To my surprise and wonder, out of her scarcity, this innocent child offered me a priceless gift. A single piece of fruit!

Soon after, You orchestrated that a believer walk five miles each day just to speak to me. Minutes into our first conversation, the man said, "I am the only Christian in my village. It's so nice to have someone to talk to about God."

Every day for weeks, the Christian man appeared by my side. Although I mostly answered his questions about what it was like to live in America, deep down, I knew that there was something special about him. I felt an unfamiliar peace and comfort in his presence. Not saved at the time, I wondered, *What kind of love prompts a person to walk five miles to speak to a complete stranger?* Were You planting a tiny seed in me?

Finally, at age 38, I surrendered my heart to Your Son, Jesus Christ. Consequently, I devoted myself to a life of prayer and service to the poor. Since I knew firsthand what the radical welcome of Christ meant to a broken and lonely heart, I began joyfully sharing the gospel with everyone You placed along my path. Now, twelve years later, I'm experiencing another unforgettable moment along "The Way."

In the world we now live in, it has become commonplace to connect with strangers over the internet. Moreover, with the current global health crisis—the COVID-19 pandemic—many are confined to their homes. It has been months since our country began practicing social distancing. In fact, people in countries all across the world have been asked to stay at home. Perhaps that is why so many people feel isolated and are reaching out for a connection, any connection, through the internet.

Last week, Your Spirit caused me to feel an overwhelming desire to swing the door of my Facebook page wide open. Remarkably, this one gesture would lead me all the way back to Africa!

Several days prior, the pages of my Bible had opened to the Book of Isaiah, chapter forty-nine. *Were You preparing me for what would come next?* I wondered. As I began to read, my eyes fixed sharply upon a few verses:

> Surely these shall come from afar;
> Look! Those from the north and the west,
> And these from the land of Sinim."
>
> Lift up your eyes, look around and see;
> All these gather together *and* come to you.
> *As* I live," says the LORD,
> "You shall surely clothe yourselves with
> them all as an ornament,
> And bind them *on you* as a bride *does*.
> (Isaiah 49:12, 18).

I had no idea then that I was about to tap into a massive population of young adults desperately wanting to know more about You. Incredibly, within one month, I had over two thousand friend requests. Many were young men still in their twenties and practicing Muslims. Incredible!

Each day, armed with faith, I opened my Facebook page to greet those who were scared, hurting, feeling lost, and in search of hope. Initially, several held out a hand, asking for money. But it didn't take long before they let their guard down and began to share their personal and intimate life stories with me. "What are you really longing for?" I asked each one. Many admitted that they were feeling lost without You and shameful for their sins.

As I read each heartbreaking story, my own redemption story came to mind. For several non-stop hours each day, I replied to countless messages. I wrote, "I will pray for Jesus Christ to comfort you. If you have not yet repented and given your life to Jesus of Nazareth, now might be a good time. God will show you that He is with you. In His love, Donna."

Remarkably, many hearts seem to lighten up. Some even seemed receptive to seeking forgiveness in Your Son, Jesus. For that reason, I began to boldly ask, "Are you ready to receive Christ into your heart?" Incredibly, every single person I asked replied, "YES!" One by one, I led each person in prayer, asking forgiveness for their sins. With each person who sincerely repented, I sobbed.

These days, a warm feeling of joy and contentment floods my soul. I feel as though I am walking on water. Today, with an outpouring of appreciative tears, I prayed,

"Oh LORD, it seems inconceivable to me that I could

have ever believed I was walking alone in this life. Ever since that miraculous day back in October 2008, when I finally surrendered my life to Your will, I've cherished my life. Knowing that You are with me each day fills my heart with peace and hope.

Thank You LORD, for Your miraculous will! Thank You for the way You lead and guide my heart upon this King's highway. Please be with each soul who has recently surrendered their heart to You. Help them to live godly lives despite pressure from their unsaved family members or peers. Father, I also thank You for reuniting me with Africa for Your glory, purpose, and your Kingdom's growth. Indeed You are sovereign over all.

Through Jesus alone, I pray. Amen."

Postscript

As I wrote this story, my heart truly began to long for Africa once again. So, I dusted off my old photo album. As I flipped the pages, I quickly discovered a handwritten letter inscribed just days before I left Mombasa, Kenya. Composed in both English and Swahili, the letter read,

> "Dear Minister.
> Goodbye minister.
> If you really love us,
> Remember us, dear.
> Do not forget us, dear.
> We will meet again."

"Mgeni mpendwa.
Kinaheri Mgeni.
Ikiwauna tupenda sisi,
Utukumbuke sisi mpendwa.
Usitusahau tutakutana tena."

Once again, You were leading me to remember Your goodness and faithfulness! Not for one moment had You forsaken me!

A few days later, my eyes welled with warm tears while reading my morning chapter of the Bible. The pages of my Bible had amazingly fallen open to Ezekiel, chapter two. In this chapter, You are calling Ezekiel to rise and receive his commission. Your Spirit had entered Ezekiel for a purpose, to make him a minister. As tears gently flowed, I thanked You for allowing me to minister to Africa and allowing Africa to minister to me.

Amen.

September 21, 2020

My Best Friend, my King, my All in All,

Today, I found myself deeply reflecting on all the ground You and I have covered together over the past twelve years. I marvel at all the people profoundly impacted by the greatness of Your love.

How could I have known that one simple prayer, prayed through a willing and open heart, would lead me to the edge of my dreams, one foot in paradise, one in the waste?

Just a few days before October 20, 2008, I prayed, "Please God, use my life to bring others to You." Amazingly, You responded! Your reply was not only miraculous but infinitely more profound and extraordinary than any I could have ever imagined!

Now, as I sit here with my torn and tattered twelve-year-old Bible resting upon my lap, I ponder the long, rugged path behind me. Over the years, I have discovered the importance of having faith in You and Your sovereign plan for my life. Indeed, Your ways are not my ways. During times when I thought a situation or task was impossible, You showed me that with You, all things are possible (Luke 18:27). When I felt too weary to carry on, You instructed me to take Your light yoke upon me and learn from Your gentleness. Afterward, You gave me rest (Matthew 11:28–30). When I felt all alone, You said,

> "Fear not, for I *am* with you; Be not dismayed,
> for I *am* your God. I will strengthen you,
> Yes, I will help you, I will uphold you with
> My righteous right hand" (Isaiah 41:10).

When I told myself nobody loved me, You reminded me that You love me. You even called me Your sister and bride (Song of Solomon). Along 'The Way,' You enlivened my prayer life, increased my faith, and lent me Your wisdom. You helped me to walk in Your love. What an incredible journey!

Oh LORD, thank You for Your grand design for my life. Thank You for leading me to remember the past few beautiful years. How sweet their memory is, still! Thank You for bringing me to this glorious mountaintop where Your grace abounds. May I always live a life wholly devoted to honoring You and bringing glory to Your name, Yahweh. Amen.

Postscript

I had just written the final entry of this prayer journal, which highlighted stories of God's infinite mercies when something surprising occurred. When I opened my Bible to spend a quiet moment with our LORD, I unexpectedly landed upon a chapter that didn't seem to fit my situation. After years of walking through deserts and having faced suffering, I had finally reached a spiritually bountiful mountaintop covered in fruit and goodness. In my mind, I had left all of my troubles far behind.

However, while on this holy summit, feeling secure, I came across a warning. Through Jeremiah chapter twelve, I felt Your Spirit instructing me to brace myself: "The worst is yet to come." My heart sunk deep into my chest. *Could this mean additional heartache was lingering around the next corner?* I wondered.

I pondered over this warning for months. Then one day, I opened that little Methodist hymnal that my dear friend had given to me a year before his passing. One prayer-filled hymn immediately caught my attention. Amazingly, the song reminded me of my entire journey thus far.

METHODIST HYMNAL 1866, #941
THE PILGRIM'S HAPPY LOT

"HOW happy is the pilgrim's lot;
How free from every anxious thought,
From worldly hope and fear!
Confined to neither court nor cell,
His soul disdains on earth to dwell,
He only sojourns here.
This happiness in part is mine,
Already saved from low design,
From every creature-love;
Blest with the scorn of finite good,
My soul is lighten'd of its load,
And seeks the things above.
There is my house and portion fair;
My treasure and my heart are there,
And my abiding home;
For me, my elder brethren stay,
And angels beckon me away,
And Jesus bids me come.
I come, thy servant, Lord, replies;
I come to meet thee in the skies,
And claim my heavenly rest!
Soon will the pilgrim's journey end;
Then, O my Savior, Brother, Friend,
Receive me to thy breast!"

The profound hymn offered clear expectations for my future as a Christian pilgrim. No matter the pain, uncertainty, loneliness, and deepest heartaches, You have a sovereign plan for my life. Moreover, You promise to go before me, always be with me, and never leave my side. (Hebrews 13:5) Thus, I can be sure that everything that happens to this pilgrim's heart is for my eternal good and for Your glory. Even my tiniest doubts and my most heart-wrenching fears are part of Your mighty plan!

"Oh LORD, I am not sure what the future holds. Yet, even if fear, trembling, and weakness cloud my path, still, I know that beyond dark skies lies the sun of your radiance, warmth, and illumination, reaching down to touch my life and every step along 'The Way.' Please LORD, help me continue to trust You as I continue my journey toward Your Father's house. Thank You for offering me fellowship with Your Holy Spirit, with Whom I have the strength to do Your will. May I never let go of Your holy hand."

And may you, dear reader, also find your pathway filled with lasting comfort and joy. May your life personify the depth of God's mercy and forgiveness towards His creation. May your love for our Savior cause you to enthusiastically share the gospel of hope with every person you meet. And may you rejoice in knowing that every step *you* take is with the Savior of the World (John 3:16).

In Jesus' name. Amen.